TO ALL THE
<u>HOME COOKS</u> OUT THERE
WHO SPEAK THE
<u>LOVE LANGUAGE</u>
OF FOOD.

THE ITALIAN HOME COOK

Silvia Colloca

plum.

Pan Macmillan Australia

CONTE

NTS

INTRODUCTION

THE KITCHEN IS THE
PLACE WHERE LIFE
HAPPENS, AND AS
WE BEAR WITNESS
TO THE PASSING
OF TIME, WE
PUNCTUATE THOSE
MOMENTS WITH THE
COMFORTING RITUAL
OF HOME COOKING.

THE KITCHEN IS WHERE LIFE HAPPENS

There is one room in my house that seems to be governed by its own gravitational laws. A place my family and I are pulled into several times a day, for different reasons. A 'room of requirement', if you will allow the Hogwarts reference, which turns into what you need when you need it most, and presents you with what you are looking for at just the right time.

It is, of course, my kitchen. A light-filled space wrapped around a bright yellow oven that invites me and my family to share meals, conversation, moments of quiet and many more moments of chaos! The kitchen is where we find ourselves if we are hungry, thirsty, bored, in need of a break, frantically packing lunchboxes, efficiently chopping ingredients for family dinners, mixing lockdown negronis ... it's the place where life happens. And as we bear witness to the passing of time, we punctuate those moments with the comforting ritual of home cooking.

Whether you are a born food lover or have inadvertently been turned into one from the 'at home' time imposed by the events of the last few years, we have all found ourselves whisking, kneading and slicing more than ever, highlighting a fundamental truth Italians have cherished for centuries: when life gets challenging, you can cook yourself happy again!

THE ITALIAN HOME COOK

If you were to ask me what is unique about Italian home cooking, I would steadfastly assert its point of difference is the cooks themselves. In breaking down the principles of Italian home cooking, we quickly learn that they are centred around four fundamental pillars – tradition, pride, creativity and simplicity – and Italians adhere to them like eggs and pecorino on carbonara! We grow up immersed in a culture that celebrates the act of cooking, and that of eating, every single day. And such reverence is offered in equal manner for a simple biscotto dunked in morning espresso, a chunky piece of bread dripping with extra-virgin olive oil or a more elaborate dish of homemade pasta.

WE ARE TAUGHT
FROM A YOUNG
AGE TO CHERISH
THE INGREDIENTS
WE COOK WITH,
WHETHER THEY ARE
HOME GROWN OR
STORE BOUGHT.

Italians have an innate respect for tradition, which is expressed with love and restraint. We don't like altering the recipes given to us by our nonnas, as if the idea alone would be enough to offend our ancestors. We maintain the customs with pride and are strongly opinionated about leaving out unnecessary ingredients, to allow the simple beauty of each dish to realise its potential. Less truly is more.

Italians are natural, inventive home cooks, but such creativity is expressed thriftily and ingeniously more than with sophistication. It takes far more imagination to cook a delicious meal out of just three or four ingredients and a wooden spoon than it does using fifteen ingredients and as many kitchen gadgets!

Above all, we are taught from a young age to cherish the ingredients we cook with. Whether they are home grown or store bought, we have observed and absorbed the actions of hands more experienced than ours caring for them with passion and knowledge, and turning them into meals that we will never stop craving or recreating, and that we will inevitably pass on to younger, hungrier hands than ours.

We have been made home cooks by the unspoken language of food, and in this book I want to share with you all that I have learned about Italian home cooking so that you can bring this rich and evocative world to life in your own kitchen. Ultimately, this book is for all of you: the accomplished home cooks, the novices, those who love kitchen gadgets and those who don't, those who look at the picture and then improvise, and those who follow the recipe to the T.

We are all home cooks. We all speak the same language, regardless of where we come from. Our language is made up of ingredients, gestures and intentions, and it tells stories of love, unity, resilience and friendship.

x Silvia

THE PANTRY IS YOUR TREASURE TROVE

Before you venture into the chapters of this book, I would love to offer you an insight into the Italian pantry. Stocking your shelves with the right ingredients is the first step to approaching cooking like an Italian. Here is my list of absolute essentials, the items I make sure I never run low on!

CANNED TOMATOES

You don't need to have a nonna providing you with a stash of passata! Stock up on good-quality canned tomatoes, either chopped or whole. As a rule of thumb, if they taste delicious from the can, your sugo has the best chance of turning into a culinary delight. Of course, if you do have the time and inclination, you can make your own passata when tomatoes are in season and at their ripest and juiciest (for a recipe, see page 28).

CANNED TUNA, ANCHOVIES AND LEGUMES

These are the most versatile ingredients you can stock in your cupboards. You can use them with pasta, on toast, in salads or to top crostini. They are ready to use and so convenient, and also add nutritional value and incredible taste. Anchovies in particular can really bring a dish to life – see pages 178–94 for my favourite ways to use this authentic Italian ingredient.

DRIED LEGUMES

While I always have cans of legumes in my cupboard for when I don't have time to cook my own, I also recommend stocking your pantry with bags of dried chickpeas and beans. Make sure to soak them overnight before boiling them the next day and using in any one of the wholesome legume recipes in this book (see pages 90–114).

DRIED PASTA AND RICE

Italians worship dried pasta. Under no circumstances do we refer to it as 'cheat's pasta'. It is a beautiful ingredient, often masterfully created, extruded through ancient bronze machines into the most incredible shapes. When in doubt, pasta is always the answer. I can't tell you how many times I have dressed plain pasta in olive oil and called it dinner. Delizioso! Rice offers as much versatility and, on the plus side, it's a wonderful gluten-free option. If you have arborio or carnaroli rice, you've got the makings for a risotto (see pages 30, 55 and 176).

EXTRA-VIRGIN OLIVE OIL

Italians use extra-virgin olive oil on virtually anything, from sweet to savoury dishes and everything in between. It is incredibly healthy as it's full of antioxidants and good fats – and it's naturally vegan, too! You can swap butter for it, if you like, but make sure you never skimp on quality when choosing your olive oil.

FLOUR AND DRIED YEAST

I always make sure I have type 00 flour and yeast in my pantry. I may not have the time to bake every day, or even once a week, but knowing it's there provides me with the comfort that, if the urge hits me, I can get kneading. From bread to pizza to brioche, it all starts with flour, yeast and a little water (see pages 228–44 for some delicious Italian bread recipes).

SALT, PEPPER AND VINEGAR

Seasoning is everything, so it's one ingredient you never want to run out of! Make sure you buy good-quality salt, pepper and vinegar. I generally use salt flakes in my cooking, as well as both black and white pepper – always freshly ground.

STOCK

My mum taught me that a good-quality stock cube and some baby pasta can turn into dinner in under 10 minutes. We call it minestrina and it's basically baby pasta cooked in stock. It's a staple in every Italian household and, in the words of my 12-year-old Miro, the best meal on earth! Add stock to your pantry, as well as a few fresh ingredients like garlic, onion, potato, lemon, herbs and parmesan cheese, and you can rest assured you will always be able to create a meal, just like an expert Italian home cook.

THE V

Nº. 1
THE VEGGIE PATCH

EGGIE

PATCH

Whether it's winter bitter greens, sweet spring peas, plump summer tomatoes or autumnal broccoli, vegetables feature proudly all year round at the Italian table. The exceptional range and variety of vegetables grown in Italy is perfectly matched by the creativity of the local home cooks, who turn them into show-stopping dishes, where the cookery skills are at the service of the ingredients, with the only intent to realise their full potential without altering or transforming their essence. Which is good news for us, because it means that to cook like an Italian you don't need any special gadgets or cheffy techniques. Just a passion for eating great food and a touch of buon senso (common sense).

The following selection of dishes is a small portion of the vast repertoire of recipes featuring vegetables that make Italian cuisine so wholesome. Some are served as sides, such as cavoletti ripassati (pan-fried brussels sprouts with chilli, see page 66), while others are the main ingredient of pasta dishes or risotto (see pages 25, 30, 41, 47, 52 and 55 for some ideas here). I have also included a few recipes for what in Italy is referred to as piatto unico, a one-plate dinner filling enough that you won't require anything else – try my melanzane alla parmigiana (eggplant, tomato and mozzarella bake, see page 71) or perhaps gattò di patate (Neapolitan potato and mortadella bake, see page 82). To kick things off, though, we celebrate the ingredient Italy is probably most famous for – il pomodoro, the golden apple, the versatile tomato!

CAPRESE CON CUORI DI BUE

(OXHEART TOMATO AND MOZZARELLA SALAD)

SERVES 4

More than a recipe, caprese is a love letter to its ingredients, showcasing their excellence in glorious simplicity. The name tells us the salad originated on the island of Capri, just off the coast of Naples; the mere thought is romantic enough to inspire me to immediately tear creamy buffalo mozzarella and chop plump, ripe tomatoes.

The choice of tomato is of fundamental importance here. End-of-summer ones, those that have spent a large part of the warm months shamelessly sun baking on their gnarly vines, are the ones to seek out. You'll know they are perfectly suited as they carry a sweet and earthy perfume. And if you can get your hands on heart-shaped heirloom tomatoes, just add salt, basil and olive oil and you will feel you are in Capri with each and every mouthful.

When it comes to oxheart tomatoes, the best way to reveal their stunning interior is to avoid cutting them into wedges, as you would with other varieties. Place the tomatoes on their side on a board and, using a small serrated knife, cut into 1 cm thick slices that resemble tomato steaks.

Place the tomato slices on a platter, tear the buffalo mozzarella into chunks and arrange on the tomato. Add the basil leaves and season with salt and pepper, then drizzle the olive oil over the top. Serve straight away with a side of focaccia or bread. I do not recommend making this salad ahead of time and keeping it in the fridge – for the reasons explained in the Note below. If taking on a picnic, slice the tomatoes and keep in a container, then arrange on a platter and season on site.

NOTE

Just as Italians never store tomatoes in the fridge (it alters both the flavour and texture), mozzarella is also kept at room temperature. Normally, I buy buffalo mozzarella with the intention to eat it that day, therefore a little time on the counter is perfect for enjoying it the way it was intended. If you buy mozzarella to have the next day or later, keep it in the fridge, but sit it at room temperature for 1–2 hours before using.

2–3 large oxheart or heirloom tomatoes or 5–6 smaller ones (impossible to give an exact quantity because nature creates distinctly unique tomatoes, no two are the same)

2 × 125 g buffalo mozzarella balls (see Note)

plenty of basil leaves

salt flakes and freshly ground white or black pepper

3–4 tablespoons extra-virgin olive oil

focaccia or crusty bread, to serve

PANE STRUSCIATO
(SMASHED TOMATO ON BREAD)

SERVES 4

1 garlic clove, cut in half (optional)

4 crusty or sourdough bread rolls,
   cut in half

4 large vine-ripened or oxheart
   tomatoes, cut in half (see Note)

salt flakes

extra-virgin olive oil (it's up to you
   how much you use, I like about
   2 teaspoons per roll)

basil leaves, to serve (optional)

Warning: this is not a recipe; pane strusciato is a way of life! I can easily live off this meal for breakfast, lunch and dinner, proudly wearing my tomato and olive oil dribbly chin.

Juicy end-of-summer tomatoes are needed here, as well as enough elbow grease to smear and smash them into submission on a cut bread roll. Season with salt flakes and olive oil, then top with some basil leaves. Bliss!

Preheat a chargrill pan to hot.

If using the garlic, rub the cut side onto the halved bread rolls. Grill the cut sides of the bread rolls on the chargrill pan for a few minutes until nice char lines appear.

Forcefully smear and squash the tomato halves onto the cut sides of the bread rolls, season with salt and olive oil. Add basil, if liked, and devour.

NOTE
When it comes to storing your tomatoes, it's essential to leave them at room temperature. The fridge dissipates all their flavour.

SPAGHETTI ALLA CRUDAIOLA

(SPAGHETTI <u>WITH</u> FRESH TOMATOES, OLIVE OIL <u>AND</u> BASIL)

SERVES 4

The act of cutting up a tomato and seasoning it with salt and olive oil also applies to pasta recipes. In fact, many hot summer nights have been saved by this clever dish, which is ready in under 10 minutes. The raw sauce is mixed together as the pasta cooks to al dente perfection. Combine the two with a little glue provided by the pasta cooking water, add some parmigiano and, magically, a creamy fresh sauce is created.

Bring a large saucepan of salted water to the boil. Drop in the spaghetti and stir to separate the strands. Cook, stirring occasionally, until al dente (generally 1 minute less than the cooking time recommended on the packet).

In the meantime, to make the sauce, place the tomato in a large bowl. Season with salt and pepper, add the olive oil, grated parmigiano and 1–2 handfuls of the basil leaves.

When the pasta is ready, lift it out with a spaghetti spoon and drop it into the bowl with the sauce, dragging a little cooking water with it. Alternatively, drain in a colander, and reserve 2–3 tablespoons of the cooking water to add to the sauce. Toss well to combine and emulsify the sauce.

Add any of the optional extras, if you like, and toss through the pasta. Divide among serving bowls, sprinkle with the remaining basil leaves and serve with extra olive oil drizzled over the top, if you like.

400 g dried spaghetti

800 g vine-ripened or roma tomatoes (in Italy we like to use San Marzano), roughly chopped

salt flakes and freshly ground white or black pepper

80 ml (⅓ cup) extra-virgin olive oil, plus extra for drizzling (optional)

35 g (⅓ cup) freshly grated parmigiano

2 large handfuls of basil leaves

OPTIONAL EXTRAS

handful of rocket leaves, torn

bocconcini, torn

chopped anchovy fillets

finely grated lemon zest

1 tablespoon pesto

LA PUMMAROLA
(HOMEMADE PASSATA)

MAKES 6 × 450 G JARS

4 kg roma tomatoes, cut in half
salt flakes, to taste
2 cups loosely packed basil leaves

STERILISING NOTES

Always use new lids. Old lids will fail to seal the jars safely.

To sterilise the jars and lids, simply put them in the dishwasher and run on a hot temperature cycle. Allow to dry in the machine.

Alternatively, wash the jars and lids in hot soapy water, rinse well and place in a stockpot. Add water to cover and boil them for 20 minutes. Lift them out with tongs and allow them to dry, upside down, on a clean tea towel.

Have you ever been tempted to make your own tomato passata, but been put off by the daunting thought that it is a complicated job, best left to the expert wrinkled hands of a good old Italian nonna? Think again! Homemade passata is within everybody's reach. All you need is a food mill, some empty glass jars and, naturally, the ripest, juiciest tomatoes you can find.

As a child growing up in Italy, I was exposed from an early age to the delicate sweetness of my mamma's and nonna's passata. Every August we children were assigned the task of washing tons of plump tomatoes, so ripe they would almost burst in our tiny, clumsy hands. Mamma and Nonna would then mill them vigorously to obtain a rich and peel-free sauce, ready to be bottled. A stash of this precious crimson nectar brightens even the coldest darkest days – making the prospect of winter a lot more endurable.

Pass the tomato through a food mill twice to make sure you extract all the juices. Season with salt, pour the freshly extracted passata into sterilised jars (see Sterilising Notes) and add a few basil leaves to each jar. Seal with new, sterilised lids.

Place the jars in a large stockpot of simmering water so that they are fully submerged. Carefully drape tea towels around them to avoid the jars bumping into each other (and breaking!). Simmer for 15 minutes then cool in the pot to allow the steam to vacuum seal the jars.

Summer in a jar is yours!

Keep the jars of passata in a dark cupboard and consume within 6 months. Once opened, store in the fridge for up to 3 days.

RISOTTO AL POMODORINO
(CHERRY TOMATO RISOTTO)

SERVES 4

The iconic Italian dish, risotto, gets a ruby makeover with the addition of tomatoes. I love using canned cherry tomatoes for this dish, their gentle softness and juiciness adds a lovely velvety texture to this bowl of comfort food your family will love. Of course, chopped tomatoes or crushed, peeled tomatoes will work well, too.

1 tablespoon extra-virgin olive oil

50 g butter

1 white onion, diced

350 g carnaroli or arborio rice

200 ml dry white wine

400 g can cherry tomatoes or chopped tomatoes

2 litres chicken or vegetable stock, brought to a gentle simmer

50 g (½ cup) freshly grated parmigiano

salt flakes and freshly ground white or black pepper

basil or thyme leaves, to serve

Heat the olive oil and half the butter in a large heavy-based frying pan over medium heat. Add the onion and cook, stirring occasionally, until softened, but not caramelised. Add the rice and stir until coated in the oil and butter.

Pour in the wine and, stirring occasionally, allow it to bubble away for 2–3 minutes or until the alcohol has evaporated. Reduce the heat to medium–low, add the tomatoes, stir well, then start adding the stock, a couple of ladlefuls at a time, giving it an occasional gentle stir. Keep adding the stock until the rice is al dente, about 16–17 minutes.

Remove the pan from the heat and add a final ladleful of stock, the parmigiano and the remaining butter. Taste for salt and adjust to your liking, then season with pepper. Stir vigorously to release the starch and create an all'onda (like a wave) texture. Cover with a lid and let it rest for a few minutes to create the perfect mantecatura (creaminess). Ladle into shallow bowls and top with some basil or thyme leaves.

POMODORI SECCHI
(OVEN-DRIED TOMATOES)

MAKES 2 X 450 G JARS

This is, quite possibly, the easiest way to recreate the flavour of Southern Italy in your kitchen. All you need are fleshy tomatoes, such as roma (in Italy we love the San Marzano variety), and your oven set on low. A few hours later your sweet bounty will be ready to stash away for when you need a summer pick-me-up.

Preheat your oven to 150°C (conventional). Line two baking trays with baking paper.

Arrange the tomato halves, cut-side up, on the trays, season with some salt and scatter the garlic on top. Bake, turning them once halfway through, for 5–6 hours or until dry and wrinkly. Discard the garlic and allow the tomato halves to cool completely on a wire rack.

Once cooled, transfer the dried tomatoes to freshly sterilised jars (see Sterilising Notes on page 28). Add the dried oregano and chilli flakes, if using, and pour in enough olive oil to completely cover the tomatoes. Seal with a lid and place in the fridge. Unopened jars will keep for 2–3 months. Once opened, use within 4 days.

Alternatively, transfer the dried tomatoes to zip-lock bags and freeze for up to 6 months. When ready to use, thaw, then soak them in warm water for 30 minutes to re-plump. Drain, pat dry with a clean tea towel and season with the olive oil, oregano and chilli flakes, if desired (no salt needed, unless you like extra).

2 kg roma tomatoes (or other plump oval-shaped variety), well washed and cut in half lengthways
salt flakes
4–5 garlic cloves, sliced
dried oregano, to taste (optional)
chilli flakes, to taste (optional)
extra-virgin olive oil (enough to cover the tomatoes)

POMODORI IMBOTTITI AL FORNO
(BAKED STUFFED TOMATOES)

SERVES 6–12
(DEPENDING ON WHETHER YOU HAVE ONE OR TWO TOMATO HALVES)

6 large vine-ripened tomatoes, cut in half crossways

100 g (1 cup) dried breadcrumbs

2 tablespoons finely chopped flat-leaf parsley

2 large handfuls of basil leaves, thinly sliced, plus extra leaves to serve

50 g (½ cup) freshly grated parmigiano

25 g (¼ cup) freshly grated pecorino

2 garlic cloves, crushed

125 ml (½ cup) extra-virgin olive oil, plus extra for drizzling

salt flakes and freshly ground white or black pepper

The love affair between Italian home cooks and tomatoes is no revelation. Since its introduction a few centuries ago, the love has grown deeper and more passionate and, it's fair to say, we are never breaking up! This humble dish is the epitome of cucina povera (peasant cooking) and one of the many creative ways Italian home cooks make use of ripe summer tomatoes.

Here, the tomatoes are hollowed out, stuffed with breadcrumbs, herbs and cheese, then baked to golden perfection. Vegetarian and full of flavour, this is great as a main dish with some greens and crusty bread on the side, as a side dish or as part of a summer picnic.

Preheat your oven to 200°C. Line a 40 cm × 30 cm baking dish with baking paper.

Scoop the pulp from the tomato halves into a bowl. Add the breadcrumbs, herbs, cheeses, garlic and one-third of the olive oil, then season with salt and pepper to your liking.

Stuff the hollowed-out tomato halves with the breadcrumb mixture, drizzle with the remaining olive oil and bake for 20–25 minutes or until golden brown on top. Finish with a drizzle of extra olive oil (chilli oil is nice too) and a scattering of extra basil leaves.

ACQUACOTTA
(TUSCAN TOMATO BROTH)

SERVES 4

If you rely on the literal translation of 'acquacotta' – cooked water – I admit this soupy concoction doesn't sound very promising. However, if you are familiar with the delicious simplicity of Italian home cooking, you'll know too well that behind this unassuming name hides a delectable dish that has been kept in cooks' repertoires over the centuries.

Acquacotta may have originated in the Middle Ages, when the local mandriani (cowboys) would cook up onions in fat, add water and bread, crack in an egg and call it dinner. Over the years tomatoes were added, giving this dish an attractive makeover, both in flavour and appearance. Think of it as poached eggs in a tomato and onion base, served with stale bread and lashings of olive oil. Always a favourite, with cowboys or regular folk.

3 tablespoons extra-virgin olive oil,
  plus extra to serve
1 large onion or 2 golden shallots,
  finely chopped
1 celery stalk, finely chopped
salt flakes and freshly ground white
  or black pepper
2 × 400 g cans peeled tomatoes,
  crushed with a fork or potato
  masher
1–2 thyme sprigs, plus extra to serve
2 tablespoons white wine vinegar
4 eggs
4 slices of stale bread, such as
  Ciabatta (see page 228)
  or sourdough

Heat the olive oil in a large heavy-based saucepan over medium heat. Add the onion or shallot, celery and a pinch of salt and cook for 3–4 minutes or until softened. Add the tomatoes, 200 ml of water and the thyme sprigs, season with salt and bring to a simmer. Cook for 20–25 minutes or until slightly reduced and thickened. Taste for seasoning and adjust to your liking.

Fill a deep frying pan with water and bring to a simmer over medium heat. Add the vinegar and stir to combine, then gently crack in an egg, swirl the water around with a spoon and poach the egg for 3 minutes for a runny yolk. Remove with a slotted spoon and drain on paper towel. Repeat to poach the remaining eggs.

Heat a chargrill pan to hot, then place the slices of bread in the pan and cook for a few minutes each side until charred. Place the bread in serving bowls, then ladle in the tomato sauce (the bread is there to soak up the sauce) and top each bowl with a poached egg. Season with a little extra salt and pepper and serve with some extra sprigs of thyme.

TORTELLI DI CAVOLO NERO E RICOTTA

(TORTELLI <u>WITH</u> CAVOLO NERO <u>AND</u> RICOTTA)

SERVES 4

Most Italian family gatherings proudly feature a large platter of homemade pasta as the table's centrepiece. In our culture that platter stands for all we hold dear in this life: family, nurture and pasta. And so, within the layers of pasta sheets coated in meaty sauce, or hidden within each and every ravioli or tortelli, we find a simple and irreplaceable gesture of affection that makes us feel special, because we know the pasta is handmade, the filling carefully prepared and the assembly of the dish attentive. Such process is a ritual that holds the heritage we are so fiercely proud of and the legacy of those who have passed it on for us to embrace.

Tortelli are the perfect entry-level preparation to the world of filled pasta, their hefty size more forgiving than dainty tortellini. A simple and classic butter and sage dressing allows for the earthy filling to really shine, and for the silky, almost see-through casing to melt in your mouth.

Place the flour on a board, make a well in the centre and drop in the eggs and 1 scant teaspoon salt. Combine using your fingers or a fork, then knead the mixture vigorously for about 10 minutes. At first it will look crumbly, but once your body heat activates the starch in the flour, the dough will change its texture, turning into a smooth, firm ball. Wrap it in beeswax wrap and let it rest in the fridge for 20 minutes.

Meanwhile, make the filling. Heat the olive oil in a large heavy-based frying pan over medium heat. Add the garlic and cook for 1 minute or until fragrant. Stir in the cavolo nero, a pinch of salt and 1–2 tablespoons water. Cover with a lid and allow the steam to wilt the cavolo nero for 2–3 minutes. Drain well and allow to cool for 10 minutes. Place the ricotta in a large bowl, add the pecorino, eggs, nutmeg, lemon zest and parsley, season with salt and pepper and mix to combine. Add the cavolo nero and mix well. Set aside.

400 g (2⅔ cups) plain or
    type 00 flour
4 eggs, at room temperature
salt flakes
coarse semolina, for dusting
freshly grated parmigiano,
    to serve

CAVOLO NERO FILLING
1 tablespoon extra-virgin olive oil
1 garlic clove, bashed with the back
    of a knife and peeled
4 cups chopped cavolo nero leaves
300 g fresh ricotta, drained
65 g (¾ cup) freshly grated pecorino
2 eggs
½ teaspoon freshly ground nutmeg
finely grated zest of 1 lemon
handful of chopped flat-leaf parsley
    leaves
freshly ground black pepper,
    to taste

BURNT BUTTER AND SAGE SAUCE
120 g butter
8–12 sage leaves

>

After the dough has rested it will feel elastic and very pliable. Dust your board with semolina, then cut the dough into quarters. Work with one piece at a time and keep the rest wrapped to prevent it from drying out. Flatten the piece of dough with the palm of your hand, then pass it through your pasta machine's widest setting three or four times, folding the dough into three each time. Continue passing the dough through the machine (no further folding required), each time through a thinner setting, until you get to the second-last setting or the sheet is roughly 2.5 mm thick.

Dust your work surface with semolina. Lay the long sheet of pasta out flat, then evenly dot heaped teaspoons of the filling down one side, making sure you leave about 3 cm between each dollop. Brush around the filling with water to moisten, then fold the sheet over and press down to seal. Gently press around each mound to remove any air bubbles (otherwise the tortelli may burst when you cook them). Cut into 5 cm squares with a pastry wheel, then place the tortelli on a tray dusted with semolina, trying not to overlap them. Repeat with the remaining dough and filling. You can cook the tortelli straight away or freeze them for up to 2 weeks.

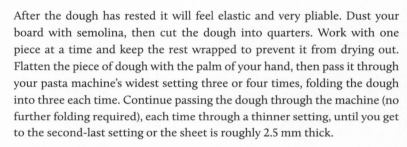

Bring a large saucepan of salted water to the boil.

Meanwhile, to make the burnt butter and sage sauce, place the butter, sage and a pinch of salt in a large heavy-based frying pan over medium heat and cook until the butter is a pale caramel colour and the sage is crispy.

Add the tortelli to the boiling water and cook for 2–3 minutes or until nicely al dente. Using a slotted spoon, lift them from the water and drop them into the burnt butter sauce. Saute for 2–3 minutes or until the tortelli are nicely coated and slightly caramelised. Season with pepper.

Arrange the tortelli on a serving platter and top with the fried sage leaves and parmigiano. Serve hot!

PIZZA DI SCAROLA
(ESCAROLE CHRISTMAS PIE)

SERVES 6

This classic Neapolitan savoury pie, packed full of bitter greens and sultanas, is traditionally made on Christmas Eve. The fact that it has very few animal products reflects how Italians still follow the religious tradition of enjoying a meat-free meal before the gargantuan feast Christmas Day brings.

Start by making the dough. Combine the flour, 150 ml of water, the yeast and olive oil in a bowl and mix until the dough comes together. Add 2 teaspoons of salt and knead lightly to incorporate. Knead on a lightly floured surface for 5–6 minutes or until a smooth, soft ball forms. Place the dough in a large bowl, drizzle over some olive oil, cover with a damp tea towel and rest at room temperature for 3–4 hours or until more than doubled in size. Knock out the air, shape back into a ball, cover and set aside until the filling is ready.

Meanwhile, to make the filling, lay the escarole or curly endive on a clean tea towel and dry well. Heat the olive oil in a large heavy-based frying pan over low heat, add the garlic, chilli flakes and anchovies, stir well and cook for 1–2 minutes or until fragrant. Add the pine nuts, olives and sultanas, stir well, then add the escarole or endive. Cover and cook for 5–8 minutes or until the escarole or endive is wilted. Taste for seasoning and adjust to your liking. Drain the excess liquid and set aside to cool for 10–15 minutes.

Preheat your oven to 200°C. Oil a 40 cm × 30 cm baking dish (or a 22 cm round springform cake tin) very well – a little extra olive oil in the base of the dish helps brown the dough.

Punch down the risen dough and knead briefly on a lightly floured surface to expel any air bubbles. Divide the dough into two portions, one slightly larger than the other. Place the larger piece of dough on your lightly floured surface and stretch by hand or with a rolling pin until 5 mm thick. Lift the dough, place it in the dish and gently press it in to line the base and sides. Spread the filling over the dough. Roll out the remaining dough until 5 mm thick, then gently place on top of the filling. Tuck in any overhanging dough and pinch the edges to seal. Using a sharp knife, cut three or four holes in the centre to allow steam to escape during baking and brush the dough with a little extra olive oil.

Bake the pie for 25–30 minutes or until golden on the top and bottom (gently lift with a spatula to make sure the base is cooked). Cool in the dish for 20–30 minutes to allow the filling to firm up a little before slicing. Enjoy warm or at room temperature.

275 g type 00 or baker's flour, plus
   extra for dusting
1 scant tablespoon dried yeast
1 tablespoon extra-virgin olive
   oil, plus extra for drizzling
   and brushing
salt flakes

ESCAROLE FILLING
500 g escarole or curly endive
   (about 2 heads), washed well and
   roughly chopped
2 tablespoons extra-virgin olive oil,
   plus extra for greasing
1 garlic clove, chopped
tip of a teaspoon chilli flakes
5–6 anchovy fillets in olive oil,
   drained and roughly chopped
100 g (⅔ cup) pine nuts
100 g (⅔ cup) pitted black olives,
   roughly chopped
100 g sultanas, soaked in water for
   30 minutes, drained and roughly
   chopped
freshly ground black pepper

ORECCHIETTE CON CIME DI RAPA

(HAND-SHAPED PASTA WITH BROCCOLI RABE)

SERVES 4

The Puglia region boasts a vast collection of recipes that Italian home cooks make on high rotation. One of the region's signature dishes is orecchiette, a type of semolina pasta that is hand-shaped into tiny rounds. Traditionally, orecchiette (literally translated as 'little ears') are paired with a sauce made of garlic, anchovies and cime di rapa – a bitter green member of the brassica family with a distinctive earthy flavour. I have a real soft spot for wintery bitter greens, so full of flavour and heavenly when pan-fried with a little garlic, chilli and olive oil. If broccoli rabe is unavailable (its winter season is short and it can be elusive to source), you can replace it with regular broccoli or even mustard greens, which are very similar in flavour.

I have given you a recipe for handmade orecchiette and, if you feel inclined to live in the skin of a pasta granny for a few hours, please give it a red-hot go, but know that most Italians tend to buy ready-made orecchiette – with no guilt whatsoever.

If you are making your own orecchiette, put the flour and salt in a large bowl, make a well in the centre and slowly pour in the water, mixing as you go to incorporate the flour. Don't add all the water at once, as you may not need it all; by the same token, you may need to add a little extra water if the dough is too stiff or dry. (Durum wheat flour may require a little more liquid than plain flour or specialty pasta flour.)

Tip the dough onto a lightly floured work surface, oil your hands and knead for 3–4 minutes or until it comes together in a smooth ball. Add a little extra flour if it feels sticky. (Alternatively, you can make the dough in a food processor. Add the water gradually and pulse the mixture instead of processing it on full speed.) Wrap it in beeswax wrap and rest in the fridge for 30 minutes. You can make the dough a day ahead, if it's more convenient.

300 g broccoli rabe (cime di rapa), trimmed

2½ tablespoons extra-virgin olive oil

4–5 anchovy fillets in olive oil, drained

1 garlic clove, thinly sliced

1 bird's eye chilli, thinly sliced, or ½ teaspoon chilli flakes

400 g dried orecchiette (if you are not making your own)

ORECCHIETTE

300 g durum wheat flour (semolina flour), plain flour or specialty pasta flour, plus extra for dusting

1 teaspoon salt flakes

220–250 ml lukewarm water

olive oil, to grease your hands

PANGRATTATO

2 tablespoons extra-virgin olive oil

100 g stale sourdough, processed to crumbs in the food processor

>

Take the dough out of the fridge, dust a board with flour and cut the dough into 4–5 pieces. Roll each piece into a 2 cm thick log, then cut into 1–2 cm pieces and generously dust with flour.

Using a butter knife, press down on a piece of dough and drag it towards you. Flip it inside out and, placing it over your thumb, shape it into a little ear. Repeat with the remaining dough, making sure you keep the board and the dough well dusted in flour. Dust the orecchiette with flour and set aside.

To make the pangrattato, heat the olive oil in a small frying over medium heat, add the breadcrumbs and toast for 3–4 minutes or until golden. Set aside.

Bring a large saucepan of salted water to the boil, drop in the orecchiette and the broccoli rabe, stir and cook for 8–9 minutes or until the pasta is perfectly al dente.

While the orecchiette and broccoli rabe are cooking, heat the olive oil in a large heavy-based frying pan over medium-low heat, add the anchovies and break them up into the oil with a wooden spoon, then add the garlic and chilli or chilli flakes and 2–3 tablespoons of pasta cooking water. Use a slotted spoon to lift the orecchiette and broccoli rabe out of the cooking water and straight into the pan, dragging a little of the cooking water with them. Stir to coat the orecchiette and broccoli rabe with the sauce. Saute for 1 minute, then spoon into bowls, top with the pangrattato and eat while hot.

ZUCCHINE E FIORI IN PASTELLA

(BATTERED <u>AND</u> FRIED BABY ZUCCHINI <u>WITH</u> THEIR FLOWERS)

SERVES 4

Zucchini are loved by Italian home cooks for their freshness and versatility. We like to slice baby ones and enjoy them raw in salads or hollow them out and stuff them with ricotta, then bake them to golden perfection. One of my favourite ways to celebrate this green vegetable and its sunshine yellow blossoms is to coat them in a light batter and deep-fry them. All that is needed is a squeeze of lemon and an ice-cold beer.

First, prepare the baby zucchini. Slice them in half lengthways and remove the stamen from each flower by gently opening up the petals and snipping it off. Set aside.

Pour enough vegetable oil into a large heavy-based saucepan to come about three-quarters of the way up the side and heat over medium heat.

Combine the flour, bicarbonate of soda and sparkling water in a shallow bowl and mix to make a sticky batter. Season with salt and pepper.

Dip the zucchini into the batter and allow the excess to drip off. Test if the oil is hot enough by dropping in a little piece of batter. If it sizzles straight away and bubbles up to the surface, the oil is ready. Working in batches, deep-fry the zucchini for 4–5 minutes or until golden and crispy. Remove with a slotted spoon and drain on paper towel. Season with salt and serve hot with lemon wedges.

12 baby zucchini with their flowers
vegetable oil, for deep-frying
250 g (1⅔ cups) plain flour or
    type 00 flour
1 teaspoon bicarbonate of soda
200 ml ice-cold sparkling water
salt flakes and freshly ground
    black pepper
lemon wedges, to serve

SPAGHETTI ALLA NERANA

(SPAGHETTI WITH A CREAMY ZUCCHINI SAUCE)

SERVES 4

Zucchini is a true 'nose to tail' vegetable, where the only discard is that small woody end where the blossom attaches itself. This garden gem goes from seedling to fruit in a matter of weeks and can be enjoyed in so many different ways – sliced in salads, stuffed, whizzed into pesto (see page 55), turned into noodles, shredded and hidden in muffin batter or pan-fried in pasta dishes such as this one. The humble zucchini may be deserving of a recipe book devoted entirely to it!

This creamy pasta dates back to the 1950s and owes its phenomenal velvety texture to the powerful combination of that holy trinity of pasta sauces: olive oil, acqua di cottura (pasta cooking water) and cheese, specifically piquant provolone. Add a generous amount of fried zucchini and you can easily see why this is a favourite in the small village of Nerano on the Amalfi Coast.

Heat 2½ tablespoons of the olive oil in a large frying pan over medium heat, add the zucchini and garlic and fry for 5–6 minutes or until nicely coloured. Season with salt and set aside. Discard the garlic.

Meanwhile, bring a large saucepan of salted water to the boil. Drop in the spaghetti and stir well to separate the strands. Cook, stirring occasionally, until al dente (generally 1 minute less than the cooking time recommended on the packet).

When the pasta is ready, return the zucchini in the pan to medium heat. Using a spaghetti spoon, transfer the spaghetti straight into the zucchini pan, dragging a little of the cooking water with it, then toss well.

Turn off the heat and add the provolone. Stir vigorously to allow the residual heat from the pan to melt the cheese and create a luscious sauce. Add the parmigiano and keep stirring until all the cheese has melted and the zucchini has broken down in the pan, creating a beautiful creaminess. Divide among bowls and serve straight away with a good grinding of pepper and a few basil leaves, if you like.

NOTE

'Alla Nerana' means 'in the style of Nerano', where this delicious pasta dish comes from.

75 ml extra-virgin olive oil

1 kg zucchini, thinly sliced

1 garlic clove, skin on, bashed with the back of a knife

salt flakes and freshly ground black pepper

400 g dried spaghetti

175 g provolone, cut into cubes

40 g freshly grated parmigiano

basil leaves, to serve (optional)

RISOTTO CON PESTO DI ZUCCHINE E RICOTTA SALATA

(RISOTTO WITH ZUCCHINI PESTO AND RICOTTA SALATA)

SERVES 4

Have you ever whizzed parboiled zucchini in a food processor and turned it into a pesto-like sauce? Mamma Mia! This emerald-green beauty is highly addictive and can easily be used as a dip as well as a pasta sauce. And on special occasions, you can turn this simple risotto into a sensational main course by topping it with zucchini flowers and shavings of ricotta salata.

To make the pesto, parboil the zucchini in salted boiling water for 3 minutes. Drain and set aside. Place the almonds, lemon zest and garlic in a food processor, add a pinch of salt and whiz until a rough paste forms. Add the zucchini, basil and olive oil and process until smooth. Add the parmigiano, mix well, then taste and adjust the seasoning. Transfer to a bowl and set aside.

Heat the oil in a large heavy-based frying pan over medium–low heat, add the leek and cook for 2–3 minutes. Add 1 ladleful of hot stock, then cover and cook for 10–15 minutes or until the leek has softened. Increase the heat to medium–high, then add the rice and stir with a wooden spoon for about 1–2 minutes or until the grains are translucent. Pour in the wine and allow it to bubble away for 2–3 minutes or until the alcohol has evaporated. Reduce the heat to medium–low and add some stock, a ladleful or two at a time, waiting until the rice has absorbed the stock before adding more. Continue adding the stock and occasionally giving it a gentle stir for 16–18 minutes or until the grains are cooked but still have an al dente bite to them.

Turn off the heat. Add the butter and half the zucchini pesto, then season to taste with salt and pepper. Stir vigorously to release the starch and create an all'onda (like a wave) texture. Cover with a lid and rest for 2–3 minutes before serving.

Ladle the risotto into shallow bowls, add 1 tablespoon of the remaining pesto and place some torn zucchini or pumpkin flowers on top. Scatter over the lemon zest and ricotta salata and serve.

NOTE

If ricotta salata is hard to find, you can use shaved pecorino instead.

2½ tablespoons extra-virgin olive oil

2 leeks, white part only, well washed and thinly sliced

1 litre vegetable stock, brought to a gentle simmer

360 g (1⅔ cups) carnaroli or arborio rice

150 ml dry white wine

25 g butter

4–5 zucchini or pumpkin flowers

finely grated zest of ½ lemon

2 tablespoons shaved ricotta salata (see Note)

ZUCCHINI PESTO

2 zucchini, cut into chunks

40 g (¼ cup) blanched almonds

finely grated zest of ½ lemon

¼ garlic clove, peeled

salt flakes and freshly ground white or black pepper

½ cup loosely packed basil leaves

3 tablespoons extra-virgin olive oil

35 g (⅓ cup) freshly grated parmigiano

CARCIOFI
(ARTICHOKES)

It is always exciting when artichokes come into season. Their presence heralds the beginning of spring, with all the spoils this time of year brings. I like to make the most of their relatively short season and prepare them in as many ways as I can. The following three dishes are my absolute favourite artichoke recipes. Admittedly, they are rather finicky to clean, but the reward is the pale chartreuse hearts, which are delicious thinly sliced and served raw with plenty of lemon juice, olive oil and parmigiano shavings (my dad's favourite), or try them steamed, pan-fried, baked or preserved in oil for winter, such is the versatility of these tasty thistles.

Here's how to prepare them. Make sure you have acidulated water at the ready and you may want to use gloves, as artichokes can stain your hands (or keep rubbing them with lemon juice as you go). As tedious as this process may sound, I always find so much beauty in watching the artichoke as it is transformed from a dark, sturdy and shielded thistle to a dainty, pale and vulnerable bud.

HOW TO PREPARE ARTICHOKE HEARTS

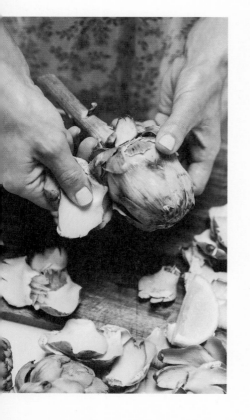

1. Working with one artichoke at a time, wash well, then trim the stalk and peel off the tough outer leaves, but keep a ring of pale green leaves around the yellow-green heart so the artichoke does not fall apart.

2. Chop off any thorns.

3. Peel the stalk.

4. Cut in half lengthways and immediately drizzle with lemon juice to prevent discolouration or rub the cut surface with a lemon half.

5. Scoop out the choke (beard) with a teaspoon to create a cavity. (If you buy the baby artichokes available at the start of the season, they barely have any choke to remove.)

6. Drop the artichoke into a large bowl of acidulated water (water with the juice of 1 lemon squeezed into it).

VIGNAROLA
(BROAD BEAN, PEA AND ARTICHOKE STEW)

SERVES 4

4 globe artichokes, prepared
(see page 56)
400 g shelled broad beans
(about 1.1 kg in their pods)
80 ml (⅓ cup) extra-virgin olive oil
4–5 spring onions, thinly sliced
150 ml dry white wine
salt flakes and freshly ground
black pepper
400 g shelled peas (about 1.1 kg
in their pods, but frozen peas
are fine)
chopped mint leaves, to serve
crusty bread, to serve

Picture this: market stalls vividly brush-stroked in emerald hues with hand-written signs saying 'fave fresche' (fresh broad beans) and 'mammole novelle' (baby globe artichokes) pointing to baskets brimming with produce. This is springtime in Rome! And savvy Roman cooks know just what to do with the greens on offer: a gentle stew with all the favourites – carciofi, fave e piselli (artichokes, broad beans and peas) – cooked with love and olive oil.

Cut the artichoke hearts into quarters and return them to the bowl of acidulated water.

Plunge the broad beans into a saucepan of boiling water for 30 seconds, then into a bowl of cold water for 30 seconds. Squeeze off their outer skins. If they are very small and young dark-green broad beans, you won't need to peel them. Set aside.

Heat the olive oil in a large heavy-based frying pan over medium–low heat. Add the spring onion and fry for 1–2 minutes or until softened. Add the artichoke, stir well, then pour in the wine and 100 ml of water and season with salt. Cover with a lid and cook, stirring occasionally, for 15 minutes. Add the peas and broad beans and cook for 4–5 minutes or until the artichoke is tender and the peas and broad beans are bright green and softened. Taste for seasoning and adjust to your liking. Add the mint and serve with lots of crusty bread.

CARCIOFI RIPIENI AL FORNO
(BAKED STUFFED ARTICHOKES)

SERVES 4–6

This preparation is very similar to carciofi alla Romana (see page 65), the main difference being the addition of pecorino, anchovies and breadcrumbs in the stuffing. The stuffed artichokes are snugly arranged in a dish and then baked until the hearts are fork tender and the stuffing is golden and crunchy. Irresistible!

Preheat your oven to 200°C. Line a baking dish just large enough to snugly fit the artichokes with baking paper.

Combine the breadcrumbs, anchovies, pecorino, herbs, garlic, 2 tablespoons of the olive oil and some salt and pepper in a bowl and mix well.

Gently prise the leaves on each artichoke half apart with your fingers, then divide the breadcrumb mixture between the leaves and cavity.

Place the artichoke halves, cut-side up, in the dish. Drizzle the remaining olive oil over the top, pour on the wine and 125 ml (½ cup) of water. Bake for 30–35 minutes or until the artichokes are golden, crunchy and fork tender. Serve hot or at room temperature.

100 g (1 cup) dried breadcrumbs

4–5 anchovy fillets in olive oil, drained and chopped

45 g (½ cup) freshly grated pecorino

⅓ cup finely chopped mint leaves

⅓ cup finely chopped flat-leaf parsley leaves

2–3 garlic cloves, finely chopped

115 ml extra-virgin olive oil

salt flakes and freshly ground black pepper

8 large globe artichokes, prepared (see page 56)

125 ml (½ cup) dry white wine

61

CARCIOFI ALLA ROMANA
(ROMAN-STYLE BRAISED ARTICHOKES)

SERVES 6

Come spring this 100 per cent vegan dish is a classic in Rome and central Italy. Typically, mammole (new-season baby artichokes) are the best-suited variety, but globe artichokes work perfectly well too. If you have leftovers, enjoy them with some bread or a side of poached eggs, or add them to a simple risotto or pasta with some pecorino – think cacio e pepe with artichokes. The season is not very long, so enjoy them while you can.

Preparing the artichokes for this recipe is simple, as we are cooking them whole. All you have do is trim the stem, pull the leaves outwards to reveal the centre, remove the chokes with a spoon to accommodate lots of fragrant stuffing, and then remove the tough outer leaves.

Combine the herbs, garlic, 3 tablespoons of the olive oil and some salt and pepper in a bowl and mix well.

Prepare the artichokes by cutting off the stem (leave about 1 cm as part of the base if you like), then gently pull the leaves apart without breaking them off, just so the choky heart is revealed. Remove the choke with a teaspoon, then remove any tougher outer leaves. Fill each cavity with the herb mixture.

Place the artichokes, stem-side down, in a saucepan just large enough to snugly fit them. Pour in water to come three-quarters of the way up the artichokes, drizzle the remaining olive oil over the top and cover with a lid. Braise over medium–low heat for 30–35 minutes or until the artichokes are tender. Serve hot or at room temperature.

½ cup finely chopped mint leaves
½ cup finely chopped flat-leaf parsley leaves
3 garlic cloves, finely chopped
150 ml extra-virgin olive oil
salt flakes and freshly ground black pepper
6–7 large globe artichokes

CAVOLETTI RIPASSATI
(PAN-FRIED BRUSSELS SPROUTS WITH CHILLI)

SERVES 4

Here's something I would like to tell eight-year-old Silvia: 'Non ci poi credere, ma da grande ti piaceranno i cavoletti di Bruxell!' ('You are not going to believe this, but you will grow to love brussels sprouts!'). Eight-year-old Silvia would probably recoil at the mere thought, but in her defence, in Italy in the 1980s, brussels sprouts and all their brassica friends used to be boiled into a grey, pungent mess that was responsible for many childhood kitchen table dramas. Mercifully, we have now learned that these green buds need very little time to cook, and preserving that crunch is the key to enjoying their nutty, slightly bitter flavour. And chilli always makes everything better!

300 g brussels sprouts

3 tablespoons extra-virgin olive oil

2 garlic cloves, peeled, bashed
    with the back of a knife

1–2 dried chillies (or use long red
    chillies, thinly sliced)

juice of ½ lemon

salt flakes

Clean the sprouts by removing the dark green outer leaves and scraping the stems with a paring knife. Cut them in half, or quarters if they are big.

Heat the olive oil in a large heavy-based frying pan over medium heat, add the garlic and chillies and cook for 30 seconds or until fragrant. Add the sprouts and pan-fry for 4–5 minutes or until slightly softened, golden brown and glistening. Turn off the heat, discard the garlic, squeeze over the lemon juice and season to taste with salt.

INVOLTINI DI VERZA AL SUGO
(STUFFED ROLLED CABBAGE LEAVES IN TOMATO SAUCE)

SERVES 4–6

This classic northern Italian dish makes good use of sturdy cabbage leaves, parboiled just long enough to become pliable and enclose a filling of mince and spring onion. The involtini (rolls) are then cooked in a simple tomato sugo. Most Italians would then apply the concept of 'cook once, eat twice': use the sauce to dress some pasta for one meal and keep the involtini for the next day. Resting the involtini overnight solidifies their flavour and texture; however, if you are not that patient, feel free to eat it all in one go. Make sure you have lots of bread to mop up the delectable sauce – this practice is called 'scarpetta' and it is almost a sacred end-of-meal ritual.

First, make the sugo. Heat the olive oil in a large heavy-based frying pan over medium heat, add the shallot and garlic and cook for 1 minute or until fragrant (watch it closely as garlic burns very quickly, especially if finely chopped). Pour in the tomatoes, then half fill the tomato can with water, swirl it around to incorporate any tomato clinging to the side, then tip into the pan. Season with salt and pepper and turn the heat to low. Add 4–5 basil leaves and simmer for 30 minutes or until reduced slightly. If it looks too dry, add a little water. Replace the wilted basil leaves with fresh ones. Set aside.

To make the involtini, bring a large saucepan of salted water to the boil. Boil the cabbage leaves for 3 minutes or until slightly soft, then drain the leaves and quickly plunge into ice-cold water to arrest cooking and preserve their vibrant green colour. Place them on a clean tea towel to dry.

Mix the mince, eggs, spring onion, pecorino, breadcrumbs, milk and parsley in a large bowl, then season with salt and pepper to your liking.

Lay a cabbage leaf on a board and trim off the thickest part of the stem. Place 2 tablespoons of the mince mixture in the middle, then roll up the leaf, tucking in the sides, as if creating a parcel. Continue until all the leaves and mince are used.

Place the involtini, seam-side down, in the pan with the sugo, trying not to overlap them. Spoon a little sugo over the top, cover and cook over medium–low heat for 25–30 minutes or until the meat is cooked (to test this, pierce an involtini with the tip of a knife, if it comes out hot, it's done). Serve hot or warm, with extra basil leaves and pecorino, if desired.

8 large outer savoy cabbage leaves

500 g pork and veal mince

2 eggs

2 spring onions, thinly sliced

65 g (¾ cup) freshly grated pecorino, plus extra to serve (optional)

2 tablespoons breadcrumbs

3 tablespoons milk

handful of chopped flat-leaf parsley leaves

SUGO

2 tablespoons extra-virgin olive oil

1 golden shallot, finely chopped

1 garlic clove, skin on, bashed with the back of a knife (or finely chopped, if you like a more pungent aroma)

400 g can peeled tomatoes (or passata or chopped tomatoes)

salt flakes and freshly ground black pepper

small handful of basil leaves, plus extra to serve (optional)

MELANZANE ALLA PARMIGIANA
(EGGPLANT, TOMATO AND MOZZARELLA BAKE)

SERVES 6

I couldn't possibly omit the mighty eggplant parmigiana – that queen of all things vegetable – from this chapter. The name of the dish is rather deceitful. One might think this vegetarian bake is named after the city Parma, in the Emilia-Romagna region ('Parmigiano' means 'from Parma'), suggesting a northern Italian origin. However, historical accounts hint to a Sicilian heritage. Eggplants were introduced to Italian soil in the 15th century by the Arabs, who at the time held dominion in Sicily. It appears that during this time local cooks made use of the strange new fruit they called 'mela insana' (bad apple) – now known as melanzana – by overlapping slices fried in lard and generously coating them with pecorino.

The addition of mozzarella and tomato has dubious origins, too. Some say those ingredients were introduced in Puglia, others attribute the genius inclusion to the creativity of cooks from Campania, such as Ippolito Cavalcanti, who featured the recipe in his 1839 book *Cucina Teorico-pratica*.

However riveting pondering the birthplace of a recipe may be, the main fact to celebrate is the recipe itself, which, in the best tradition of Italian recipes, has been pretty much left untouched since the early 1800s. So, if you are wondering whether you should add some chicken to this dish, or maybe pesto, think again! Very much like gattò di patate (see page 80), parmigiana is considered a piatto unico (only course). Think of it as a virtuous gluten-free vegetarian lasagna.

Start by preparing the eggplants. If you are using eggplants at the peak of the season, simply cut and fry them straight away. However, if they contain a lot of seeds, you will need to salt them first to remove moisture and bitterness. To do this, cut the eggplants into 1 cm thick slices. Sprinkle the slices with cooking salt and firmly pack together in a colander. Transfer the colander to the sink, then place a small plate on top and weigh it down with something heavy (a few cans of beans work well). This process encourages the water, along with any bitterness, to be released from the eggplant. Leave for about 30 minutes. Brush off the salt and pat each slice dry with paper towel. As tedious as these steps are, they ensure the eggplant slices will fry beautifully, without becoming soggy.

1.5 kg eggplants (about 4 medium-sized ones)
olive oil, for deep-frying
plain flour, for dusting
2 × 250 g mozzarella balls, thinly sliced
35 g (⅓ cup) freshly grated parmigiano
a few small cubes of butter
basil leaves, to serve

SUGO

2 tablespoons extra-virgin olive oil
1 golden shallot, finely chopped
1 garlic clove, skin on, bashed with the back of a knife (or finely chopped, if you like a more pungent aroma)
2 × 400 g cans peeled tomatoes (or passata or chopped tomatoes)
salt flakes and freshly ground black pepper
small handful of basil leaves, plus extra to your liking ('more is more' in this case!)

>

Pour enough olive oil into a large heavy-based saucepan to come about three-quarters of the way up the side and heat over medium–high heat. Test if the oil is hot enough by dropping in a small piece of eggplant. If it floats to the surface straightaway and sizzles, the oil is ready. Working in batches, dust the eggplant slices in the flour, shake off the excess, then drop them into the hot oil. Fry for 2–3 minutes on each side or until golden. Lift out with a slotted spoon, drain on paper towel and set aside.

To make the sugo, heat the olive oil in a large heavy-based frying pan over medium heat, add the shallot and garlic and cook for 1 minute or until fragrant (watch them closely as garlic burns very quickly, especially if finely chopped). Pour in the tomatoes, then half fill the tomato cans with water, swirl around to incorporate any tomato clinging to the side, then tip into the pan. Season with salt and pepper and turn the heat to low. Add 4–5 basil leaves and cook for 30 minutes or until reduced slightly. If it looks too dry, add a little water. Replace the wilted basil leaves with fresh ones. Set aside.

Preheat your oven to 200°C.

Cover the base of a 40 cm × 30 cm baking dish with a few tablespoons of sugo. Add a layer of eggplant, ladle on some sugo, top with some mozzarella and parmigiano, then scatter over a few basil leaves. Repeat until you run out of ingredients, finishing with a layer of parmigiano and dotting on the butter. Bake for 20 minutes or until golden and bubbly on top. Allow to cool for 30 minutes before serving (this allows it to firm up a little and will make cutting the portions a lot easier). Top with some fresh basil leaves and serve.

PASTA ALLA NORMA
(PASTA <u>WITH</u> FRIED EGGPLANT)

SERVES 4

When it comes to Italian icons, pasta and opera spring to mind, and this Sicilian dish marries the two brilliantly. Legend has it that pasta alla Norma was first created to celebrate the world premiere of Bellini's masterpiece. If you ever feel like indulging, try enjoying every mouthful while listening to Maria Callas singing Norma's most memorable aria, 'Casta Diva'...shivers!

For this recipe it's best to use summer eggplants at the peak of the season, as they won't need any salting to remove bitterness. Alternatively, use the method for salting eggplant on page 71. Ricotta salata (salted dry ricotta) is shaved on top to finish and, to be honest, there is nothing that comes near its unique flavour, so try to find a reputable Italian deli to source this elusive ingredient. If in dire straits, shavings of pecorino romano can be used (just don't tell any Sicilians!).

Cut the eggplants into 2–3 mm thick rounds (if using bigger eggplants, cut them into four and slice into thin wedges). Pour enough olive or vegetable oil into a heavy-based saucepan to come three-quarters of the way up the side and heat over medium heat. Test if the oil is hot enough by dropping in a small piece of eggplant. If it floats to the surface straightaway and sizzles, the oil is ready. Fry the eggplant slices, in batches, for 1–2 minutes each side. Lift out with a slotted spoon, drain on paper towel and set aside.

Heat the extra-virgin olive oil in a large heavy-based frying pan over medium heat, add both the chopped and bashed garlic cloves and stir to prevent from burning. After 30 seconds, or when it smells fragrant but is still pale, add the tomatoes and 200 ml of water. Half fill the tomato can with water and swirl around to incorporate any tomato clinging to the side, then pour into the sugo. Season with salt and pepper and bring to a simmer. Turn the heat to low, cover and cook gently for 30–40 minutes or until slightly reduced.

Bring a large saucepan of salted water to the boil, drop in your pasta and stir well. Cook until almost al dente (generally 1 minute less than the cooking time recommended on the packet). Using a slotted spoon, lift the pasta straight into the sugo pan, dragging a little of the cooking water with it. Toss well to coat every single bit of pasta.

Season the eggplant with salt, add half to the sugo and stir. Divide among bowls, top with the remaining eggplant, a few basil leaves, freshly ground pepper and lashings of ricotta salata. Sing 'Casta Diva' as you slurp (optional).

400 g small, oval-shaped eggplants

olive oil or vegetable oil, for deep-frying

2 tablespoons extra-virgin olive oil

2 garlic cloves, 1 finely chopped, the other peeled and bashed with the back of a knife

400 g can peeled or chopped tomatoes

salt flakes and freshly ground black pepper

400 g dried short pasta (such as fusilli, penne rigate or rigatoni)

basil leaves, to serve

150 g freshly shaved ricotta salata

PEPERONATA CON PANE BRUSCATO

(SWEET AND SOUR CAPSICUM STEW)

SERVES 4

Peperone (capsicum) arrived on Italian soil aboard the large ships that explored South America around 500 years ago and it is the emblem of Southern Italian cuisine. Its versatility in the kitchen is such that it can be enjoyed raw in salads, or charred, peeled and dressed lavishly with olive oil. It can be stuffed and baked (see page 79) and even a small piece of it can flavour a simple tomato sauce with the taste of the Italian summer (see page 130). For a capricious twist of faith, capsicum lacks the spice of its cousin, peperoncino (chilli), making it well loved by foodies of all ages.

I will admit that nothing comes close to my mum's peperonata. Her version of this sweet and slightly sour capsicum stew is the finest expression of Italian creativity: the fruit is treated to the company of olive oil, salt and vinegar and loudly declared one of Italy's signature dishes. Serve hot, warm, cold and even fridge cold . . . it has cured many hangovers in my lifetime, which must be due to the capsaicin in the capsicum, a compound that is known as nature's pain relief!

Heat the olive oil in a large heavy-based frying pan over medium heat, add the shallot and garlic and cook for 2–3 minutes or until the shallot has softened and the garlic smells fragrant. Add the capsicum, vinegar, sugar and a pinch of salt and cook for 1–2 minutes. Pour in the tomatoes, then reduce the heat to low, cover with a lid and stew gently for 20–25 minutes. Remove from the heat and discard the garlic.

Preheat a chargrill pan over high heat until hot.

To make the garlic toast, rub both sides of the bread slices with the cut sides of the garlic, then brush each side with the olive oil. Season well with salt and place in the chargrill pan for 2–3 minutes each side or until crunchy and grill marks have formed.

Top the peperonata with a few basil leaves and serve with the garlic toast.

3 tablespoons extra-virgin olive oil
4 golden shallots, thinly sliced
2 garlic cloves, skin on, bashed with the back of a knife
5 capsicums (red, yellow or green), deseeded and cut into strips
3 tablespoons white balsamic vinegar
1–1½ tablespoons caster sugar, or to taste
salt flakes
250 g (1 cup) canned crushed tomatoes
basil leaves, to serve

GARLIC TOAST
4 slices of stale sourdough or Ciabatta (see page 228)
2 garlic cloves, peeled and cut in half
80 ml (⅓ cup) extra-virgin olive oil

PEPERONI RIPIENI
(BAKED STUFFED CAPSICUMS)

SERVES 4

Stuffing and baking vegetables is very popular in Italian kitchens. It's a crafty way to extend the life of vegetables that have been left neglected in the fridge for a day too long and need a little revamp. Filling them with a tomato and mince mixture is definitely going to give your vegetables a tasty makeover, but of course, this recipe works just as well with freshly picked, freshly bought peperoni (capsicum). I have a personal preference for the yellow ones, plump and slightly sweet yet carrying just enough tartness to become the perfect vessel for its saucy ripieno (filling).

Heat the olive oil in a large frying pan over medium heat, add the onion, celery and carrot and saute for about 2 minutes. Add the garlic and cook for 1 minute, watching it closely as it can burn. Stir in the mince, breaking up any lumps with a wooden spoon, then increase the heat to high and cook for 3–4 minutes or until evenly browned. Deglaze the pan with the wine, scraping up any pieces caught on the base, and allow it to bubble away for 2–3 minutes or until the alcohol has evaporated.

Add the passata and 150 ml of water to the pan, then reduce the heat to low and bring to a simmer. Cook gently for 30 minutes or until the liquid is mostly absorbed. Set aside to cool slightly.

Preheat your oven to 200°C. Grease and line a large baking dish with baking paper. Pour 125 ml (½ cup) of water into the dish – once in the oven, the water will create steam that will help to cook the capsicum through.

Cut the stalks off the capsicums and scoop out the seeds and membrane. Add the herbs, pecorino and breadcrumbs to the meat mixture and stir well to combine. Divide the filling evenly among the capsicums. Top with extra breadcrumbs and a drizzle of olive oil and season with salt and pepper. Place the capsicums in the dish and bake for 30 minutes or until golden. Serve topped with parsley leaves, if you like.

3 tablespoons extra-virgin olive oil,
   plus extra for drizzling
1 onion, finely chopped
1 celery stalk, thinly sliced
1 carrot, finely chopped
2 garlic cloves, finely chopped
300 g pork and veal mince
150 ml dry white wine
400 g passata
4 capsicums (red, yellow or green)
3 tablespoons finely chopped
   flat-leaf parsley leaves
1 tablespoon finely chopped chives
60 g (⅔ cup) freshly grated pecorino
65 g (⅔ cup) dried breadcrumbs,
   plus extra to top each capsicum
salt flakes and freshly ground
   black pepper
baby flat-leaf parsley leaves,
   to serve (optional)

GATTÒ DI PATATE
(NEAPOLITAN POTATO AND MORTADELLA BAKE)

SERVES 4–6

If you are strong enough to resist a cake made of mashed potato and melted cheese, then congratulations to you. I have made peace with my weaknesses and fully accept that I can no longer refuse the temptation of the Neapolitan potato cake, gattò di patate. (The term gattò comes from gateau, the French word for cake.) This is one of those dishes we refer to as piatto unico (only course), as it is truly filling; however, you can portion it out with some prudence and enjoy it as a rich side dish.

Cook the potatoes in a saucepan of boiling salted water until tender. Drain and, when the potatoes are cool enough to handle, peel. If you have a potato ricer, you can pass them through the press without peeling them; if you don't have a potato ricer, place the cooled, peeled potatoes in a bowl and mash until smooth. Add the butter, parmigiano, nutmeg, egg and salt to taste. Mix well and set aside to cool slightly.

Preheat your oven to 200°C. Carefully grease a 20 cm pie dish with butter and coat with 1 handful of the breadcrumbs.

Arrange half the potato mixture in the dish and flatten with a spoon. Add the mortadella and provolone, then top with the remaining potato mixture. Sprinkle the remaining breadcrumbs on top and dot on a few small cubes of butter. Bake for 30 minutes, or until the top looks golden brown and crispy. Serve hot, warm (easier to portion out) or at room temperature.

700 g red potatoes, unpeeled

20 g butter, plus extra for greasing and dotting on top

35 g (⅓ cup) freshly grated parmigiano

¼ teaspoon freshly ground nutmeg

1 egg

salt flakes

2–3 handfuls of dried breadcrumbs

70 g mortadella (ask your deli to slice it 1 cm thick), cut into 1 cm cubes

70 g provolone, cut into cubes

PATATE AL FORNO ALLA ROMANA

(ROMAN-STYLE ROAST POTATOES WITH CHERRY TOMATOES)

SERVES 4–6

5 red potatoes, peeled and cut into
  3–4 mm thick slices
300 g cherry tomatoes, cut in half
80 ml (⅓ cup) extra-virgin olive oil
salt flakes and freshly ground
  black pepper
1–2 tablespoons dried oregano
oregano leaves, to serve (optional)

The only rule I live by when roasting potatoes is to make more than I think will be needed. The humble tuber steals the show when accompanying any sort of roast, to the point that I often have it on its own as the main event. Add a side salad and a glass of soave and you are dreaming of Italy. Any leftovers are amazing in a frittata.

Preheat your oven to 220°C. Line a large baking tray with baking paper.

Place the potato slices and tomato halves in a bowl. Drizzle over the olive oil and mix with your hands to evenly coat everything. Season with salt and pepper and sprinkle on the oregano.

Spread the potato and tomato on the tray and bake for 30–35 minutes or until golden and delicious. Top with oregano leaves, if desired, and serve.

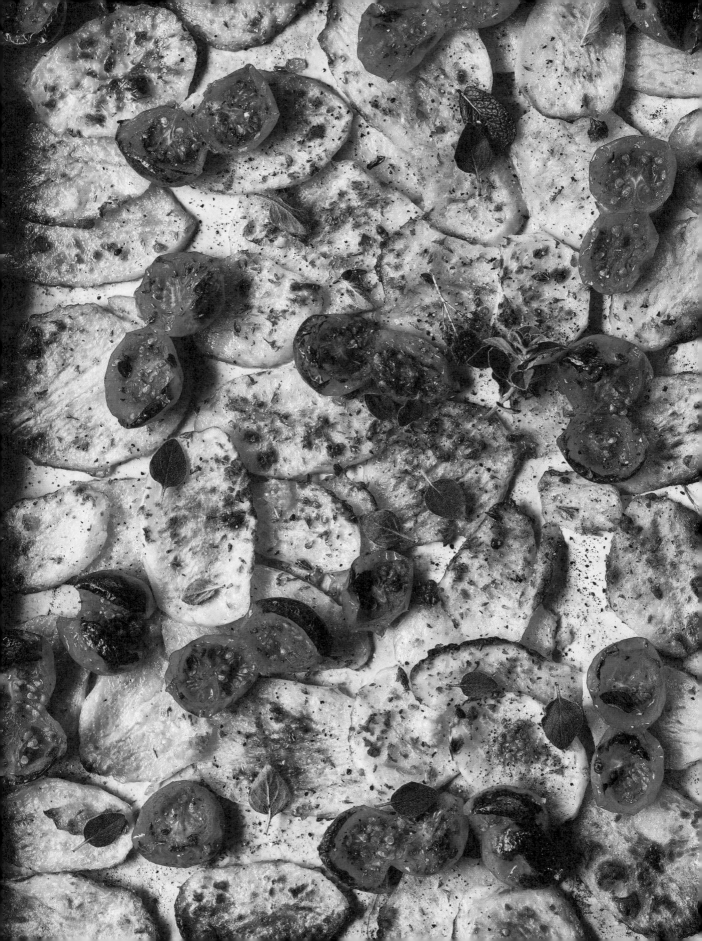

ROSE'S ZEPPOLE CON PATATE E ACCIUGHE
(SAVOURY POTATO DOUGHNUTS)

SERVES 6–8 (MAKES 15–20)

My dear friend Vitina's mum, Rose, is the authority on these golden nuggets. She is known to churn out endless batches to satisfy her family's demands at Christmas time. With the exception of one time, when Rose thought she'd give zeppole-making a miss . . . and her nearest and dearest spiralled into a festive tantrum. The lesson was quickly learned, and no Christmas day has gone by since then without large platters of zeppole being offered to grandi e piccini (the old and the young)! Rose's secret weapon in these savoury zeppole is potato, cooked and mixed in with the flour, eggs, yeast and milk. For an added surprise inside, each savoury doughnut is stuffed with an olive or anchovy fillet before frying.

Cook the potatoes in a saucepan of boiling salted water until tender. Drain and, when the potatoes are cool enough to handle, peel. If you have a potato ricer, you can pass them through the press without peeling them; if you don't have a potato ricer, place the cooled, peeled potatoes in a large bowl and mash until smooth. Add the eggs and stir until well combined.

Combine the yeast and milk in a small bowl, then add to the potato mixture with the flour and stir until the dough starts to come together. Add a good pinch of salt and knead until a smooth dough forms. If it looks too dry, add a little more milk; or if too wet, add a little extra flour, but keep in mind that a wetter dough will yield fluffier zeppole. Cover the bowl with a damp tea towel and set aside at room temperature for 2 hours or until the dough is doubled in size.

Pour enough olive or vegetable oil into a large heavy-based saucepan to come three-quarters of the way up the side and heat over medium heat. Test if the oil is hot enough by dropping in a little piece of dough. If it sizzles straight away and bubbles up to the surface, the oil is ready.

Working in small batches, pinch off golf ball–sized pieces of dough, stuff each with an anchovy or olive (or both!) and drop them into the hot oil. Cook for 3–4 minutes or until golden and puffed up. (Do not overcrowd the pan or the oil temperature will drop, causing your zeppole to absorb too much oil.) Lift out with a slotted spoon, drain on paper towel and serve hot.

500 g red potatoes, unpeeled
2 eggs
7 g sachet dried yeast
80 ml (⅓ cup) milk
500 g (3⅓ cups) type 00 flour
salt flakes
olive oil or vegetable oil, for deep-frying
anchovy fillets and/or pitted olives, for stuffing

LEGUM

N°. 2
LEGUMES & GRAINS

&   G

ES

RAINS

Although it is true that the iconic picture of Italian home cooking would most likely feature a generous bowl of spaghetti al pomodoro as the country's signature dish, everyday cuisine is made of so much more. Italian home cooks love to stock their pantries with dry foods like legumes and grains, knowing these convenient goods will provide a wide range of exciting meals. The repertoire of recipes in which these ingredients are used is as vast as it is delicious: legumes, such as lentils, beans and chickpeas, and grains like spelt and barley are prominent in most regional cuisines, highlighting a fundamental truth about Italian home cooking: it is virtuous and nutritious.

Ceci (chickpeas) are mostly used in their pure form, often stewed along with onion and garlic, sometimes roasted to a mouth-watering crunch. But it is when they are ground into flour that they reveal their show-stopping potential, turning into panelle (Sicilian fritters, see page 90) or farinata (Ligurian flatbreads, see page 92).

Lenticchie (lentils) are passionately loved by the intrinsically parsimonious Italian because they are said to bring money, and no Italian would be caught not scoffing down a bowl of the dark, pebble-like seeds on New Year's Eve when the wish for riches is cast. How lucky that they taste so good too.

Fagioli (beans) enjoy the most acclaim, their creamy texture and gentle flavour winning accolades with children, the harshest food critics around. Take it from my nephew Valerio, who could happily devour a bowl of tasty and economical pasta e fagioli (pasta and bean soup) every single day. So savvy at eleven years of age.

Farro (spelt) and orzo (barley) are nutrient-dense grains with little fat, high in both fibre and protein, making them suitable candidates for soups and salads. Orzo can also be used as a rice substitute for risotto recipes, its satisfying chewiness needing a little extra cooking time though. Orzo is sold as barley or pearl barley, the only difference between the two being that pearl barley is not a wholegrain and it's less nutritious as it's lost its outer husk and bran layer. Other than that, they are pretty much interchangeable when it comes to cooking methods.

And just to be clear orzo (barley) is not to be mistaken with the pasta shape of the same name, which I know makes matters a little confusing. I can only think that when they named that particular baby pasta, they thought it would be fitting to call it orzo, as the grain is a similar shape, just as farfalle, another pasta shape, is named after bow ties, for the same reason.

PANELLE
(SICILIAN FRITTERS)

SERVES 4–6

Panelle are an iconic Sicilian street food, traditionally sold from trucks on the side of dusty, prickly-pear-adorned roads. They merely consist of chickpea flour and water cooked into a polenta-like mixture that is then set, cut into squares and fried. They can, of course, be flavoured with herbs or chilli, and need a generous squeeze of lemon to complement their nutty taste. You can serve them cut into squares as a vegan aperitif or, as the locals of Sicily do, stuff them into warm bread rolls. Bedda Madre!

Whisk the chickpea flour and 800 ml of water in a saucepan until lump free. Season with salt and pepper, stir through the herbs and chilli flakes (if using) and place over medium–low heat. Cook, stirring constantly as if making polenta, for 4–5 minutes or until creamy and thickened to a polenta-like consistency. Turn off the heat.

Spread the mixture onto an oiled, non-stick 40 cm × 30 cm tray until about 3 cm thick. Cover with a tea towel or beeswax wrap and allow to set at room temperature for 1–2 hours (you can also do this the day before and set in the fridge overnight). Cut the set panelle mixture into 4–6 portions.

Pour enough olive or vegetable oil into a large heavy-based saucepan to come three-quarters of the way up the side and heat over medium heat. Test if the oil is hot enough by dropping in a little piece of panelle. If it sizzles straight away and bubbles up to the surface, the oil is ready. Add the panelle in batches and deep-fry for 1–2 minutes or until crispy and golden. Drain on paper towel and season with salt and pepper.

To serve, stuff each bread roll with a panella (singular for panelle), squeeze a little lemon juice on top and add a few spinach leaves and pickled vegetables, if desired.

250 g (2¼ cups) chickpea flour
 (besan)
salt flakes and freshly ground
 black pepper
1–2 tablespoons chopped herbs
 (such as flat-leaf parsley and
 basil; optional)
½ teaspoon chilli flakes (optional)
olive oil or vegetable oil,
 for deep-frying

TO SERVE
crusty or sourdough bread rolls
lemon wedges
baby spinach leaves (optional)
pickled vegetables (optional)

FARINATA DI CECI
(LIGURIAN CHICKPEA PANCAKES)

SERVES 4–6

This savoury flatbread is typical of the Ligurian shores, where it's known as faina, and it's so popular the small villages of the region boast dedicated botteghe (little shops) that specialise in churning out large trays of this delicacy from dawn until dusk. Much like Sicilian panelle (see page 90), they are the result of mixing chickpea flour with water and olive oil. The mixture is then poured onto round trays and baked in wood-fired ovens. In this version, adapted for eager home cooks willing to try this traditional food, your stove top and a non-stick pan will do. Ultimately, it's those crunchy edges you are after. Once cut into wedges and seasoned with salt flakes, faina can be enjoyed as it is or as part of a sharing course with prosciutto, salami and cheese.

Pour the warm water into a bowl and slowly whisk in the chickpea flour until smooth. Add 1 tablespoon of salt and the extra-virgin olive oil and skim any foam off the surface using a slotted spoon. Stand at room temperature for at least 4 hours, or overnight. This will allow the batter to bloom slightly and develop in texture and flavour.

Heat a 24 cm cast-iron or non-stick frying pan over medium–high heat and add 2 tablespoons of olive oil, swirling to coat the base evenly. Pour in enough batter so that it's about 5 mm thick. Cook for 3–4 minutes, then flip the pancake and cook for a further 1–2 minutes or until golden. Slide onto a plate, then repeat with the remaining batter to make three large pancakes.

Slice the pancakes into wedges and serve warm or at room temperature with your choice of salami, prosciutto or cheese.

350 ml warm water

250 g (2¼ cups) chickpea flour (besan)

salt flakes

3 tablespoons extra-virgin olive oil

freshly ground white pepper

olive oil, for pan-frying

salami, prosciutto or cheese, to serve

CECI IN UMIDO ALLA DIAVOLA
(SPICY CHICKPEA STEW)

SERVES 4

This is one of the most versatile recipes Italian home cooks swear by. You can apply the same method to beans as well (also lentils, minus the soaking part), as legumes do love a good, slow stew in an onion, pancetta and bay leaf–flavoured broth. Once cooked, they can be enjoyed as a side dish, accompanying fried eggs or bitter greens, or they can be served with pasta, making a more substantial piatto unico (only course).

If you are using dried chickpeas, soak them in plenty of water overnight. The next day, drain the chickpeas, then place them in a saucepan and cover with water. Simmer, topping up with more water if needed, for 45–60 minutes or until tender. Drain and set aside.

Heat the olive oil in a large heavy-based saucepan over medium heat, add the pancetta or speck, cheese rind, spring onion and bay leaves and cook for 1–2 minutes. Stir in the garlic and chilli and cook for 1 minute or until fragrant. Add the chickpeas, pour in the stock and simmer for 15–20 minutes or until the stock has reduced by one-third. Remove the cheese rind, taste for salt and adjust accordingly, then top with extra chilli, if you like.

Serve as a side dish, or enjoy on its own, drizzled with extra olive oil.

440 g (2 cups) dried chickpeas or
   2 × 400 g cans chickpeas, well
   drained
3 tablespoons extra-virgin olive oil,
   plus extra for drizzling
2 cm thick piece of pancetta or speck
   (about 50 g), cut into 2 cm cubes
   (omit for a vegetarian option)
small piece of pecorino or
   parmigiano rind
4–5 spring onions, thinly sliced
1–2 bay leaves
1 garlic clove, finely chopped
1 small red chilli, finely chopped,
   plus extra to serve (optional)
1 litre chicken or vegetable stock
salt flakes

CECI CROCCANTI CON SPEZIE
(ROASTED CHICKPEAS WITH SPICES AND HERBS)

SERVES 4 AS A SNACK

If you haven't tried this addictive snack yet, I vehemently invite you to do so quickly! I am not sure who came up with the idea of roasting dried and soaked chickpeas, but that person is a certified genius. Just when you thought they couldn't be more fabulous, with their creamy, velvety bite, someone thought to add a little crunch to the mix – and it's bellissimo!

The principle is simple: soak your chickpeas overnight, then drain and remove all the moisture, season with salt and lots of olive oil and roast until crispy and golden. At this point, add your favourite flavourings – in my case a herb, lemon and chilli combination. Serve hot!

You'll need to start this recipe a day ahead.

Preheat your oven to 220°C. Grease a large baking tray.

Drain the chickpeas well, then dry thoroughly with paper towel. Place them in a bowl and toss with the olive oil and salt.

Transfer the chickpeas and oil to the prepared tray and transfer to the oven to roast for 30–35 minutes or until golden brown and crunchy. Remove from the oven and immediately season with the oregano, lemon zest and chilli flakes. Place them in a serving bowl and serve straight away to enjoy the crunch. (After a while, the crunch will subside and the chickpeas will become creamy and nutty, which is still rather divine, but if you are after a crispier finish, just pop them back in the oven for 10–15 minutes.)

NOTE
You can also use canned chickpeas, just make sure you drain them well and dry them thoroughly.

440 g (2 cups) dried chickpeas, soaked overnight in plenty of water until doubled in size
80–100 ml extra-virgin olive oil
salt flakes
1 tablespoon dried oregano
finely grated zest of 1 lemon
1 teaspoon chilli flakes

ZUPPA DI GNOCCHETTI E LENTICCHIE

(LENTIL AND SEMOLINA GNOCCHI SOUP)

SERVES 4

As a child I was never too thrilled at the sight of lenticchie (lentils). No matter what magic Mum's cookery conjured up, the sight of these dark-brown legumes would instantly break the spell for me. Unless, of course, pasta was added to the concoction . . . then I would devour a scalding bowl and put my hand up for seconds or thirds. Somehow the starchy contribution made the meal more appealing to my unrefined palate, especially if semolina gnocchetti were rolled and added. A dusting of parmigiano and a drizzle of olive oil to make this robust dish shimmer are all that's needed to win the favour of children and grown-ups alike. In a twist of events, all of my children are avid lentil eaters, and they are often content to scoff a bowl of these nutrient-packed seeds with no pasta in sight—showing me once again how the next generation always has the upper hand in the evolution game. You can use this base and swap the lentils for soaked and boiled (or canned) chickpeas or beans, too. You might want to bookmark this recipe.

First make the gnocchetti. Put the flour and a pinch of salt in a large bowl, make a well in the centre and slowly pour in 220 ml of water, mixing as you go to incorporate it with the flour. Don't add all the water at once, as you may not need it all. Tip the dough onto a floured surface, oil your hands and knead for 3–4 minutes or until it comes together in a smooth ball. Add a little extra flour if the dough feels a bit wet. Wrap it in beeswax wrap and let it rest in the fridge for 30 minutes.

Remove the dough from the fridge and divide into 8–10 balls. Roll each ball into a 1 cm thick rope, then cut into 5 mm pieces. Take one piece at a time and roll it along the tines of a fork or over a wooden gnocchi board to form ridges. Dust with flour and set aside.

---

3 tablespoons extra-virgin olive oil, plus extra for drizzling

3 golden shallots or 1 onion, roughly chopped

1 celery stalk, thinly sliced

1 carrot, chopped

2 cm thick piece of pancetta or speck (about 50 g), cut into 2 cm cubes

200 g (1 cup) puy lentils, rinsed under cold water

1 tablespoon tomato paste

small piece of pecorino or parmigiano rind

1–2 thyme sprigs

750 ml (3 cups) vegetable or chicken stock, plus extra if needed

salt flakes and freshly ground black pepper

500–750 ml (2–3 cups) boiling water

freshly grated pecorino, to serve

thinly sliced small red chillies, to serve (optional)

GNOCCHETTI

430 g (2 ½ cups) durum wheat flour (semolina flour), plus extra for dusting (if hard to find, use type 00 flour)

salt flakes

>

99

Heat the olive oil in a large heavy-based saucepan over medium heat, then add the shallot or onion, celery and carrot and cook for 3–4 minutes or until the vegetables are softened but not coloured. Stir in the pancetta or speck and cook for 2–3 minutes, then add the lentils, tomato paste, cheese rind, thyme, stock and a pinch of salt and simmer over medium–low heat for 25–30 minutes or until the lentils are almost cooked through.

Add the gnocchetti to the lentils and pour in enough boiling water to cover, then cook for 5–6 minutes or until the gnocchetti is al dente and the lentils are tender. You will notice that the natural starch in the gnocchetti acts as a thickener, so add a little more stock or water if you prefer a more liquid soup. Remove the cheese rind, then season to taste with salt and pepper.

Ladle the soup into bowls and finish with a drizzle of olive oil and some grated pecorino. Serve with sliced red chilli, if desired.

NOTES
You can make the lentil soup the day before you need it. The next day, add 250 ml (1 cup) of water and a pinch of salt, then bring to the boil and cook the gnocchetti as instructed in the recipe.

You can use store-bought pasta, like ditalini or risoni, instead of the gnocchetti.

INSALATA DI VERDURE ARROSTO E LENTICCHIE

(ROAST VEGETABLE AND LENTIL SALAD)

SERVES 4

4 parsnips, peeled and cut into
   quarters lengthways
1 bunch of Dutch or heirloom baby
   carrots, scrubbed, cut in half
   lengthways, scrubbed
1 swede, peeled and cut into wedges
1 fennel bulb, cut into 5 mm thick
   slices, fronds and green stalks
   reserved
a few garlic cloves, skin on, bashed
   with the back of a knife
3–4 tablespoons extra-virgin
   olive oil
salt flakes and freshly ground
   black pepper
200 g (1 cup) puy lentils, rinsed
   under cold water

HERB AND ALMOND DRESSING
handful of basil leaves
handful of flat-leaf parsley leaves
2 tablespoons chopped fennel
   fronds
2–3 handfuls of almonds
75 ml extra-virgin olive oil
juice of ½ lemon

This highly nutritious salad is proof of how virtuous Mediterranean-style cooking is, as it is both gluten free and vegan, but not shy of bold flavours provided by the lentils, fennel and root vegetables. I find that roasting is a very forgiving way to give extra life to vegetables that may have been neglected in the fridge for a few days too many … something the parsimonious Italian home cook in me truly appreciates.

Preheat your oven to 200°C. Line a baking tray with baking paper.

Toss the vegetables and garlic with the olive oil in a bowl, season with salt and pepper, then tumble onto the tray. Roast, stirring occasionally, for 30–35 minutes or until the vegetables are golden and cooked through.

In the meantime, cook the lentils in a saucepan of salted boiling water until al dente, about 30 minutes. Drain and set aside.

Place the herb and almond dressing ingredients in a food processor. Roughly chop some of the reserved green fennel stalk, add it to the processor and blitz until the mixture resembles a runny pesto. Set aside.

To assemble the dish, transfer the lentils to a platter, top with the vegetables, drizzle the dressing over the top and gently toss, then scatter over the reserved fennel fronds.

PIATTONI AL SUGO
(ITALIAN FLAT BEANS IN TOMATO SAUCE)

SERVES 4

Piattoni al sugo is an Italian classic! Nutritious and delicious, I often just enjoy it with some crusty bread, but it can also be a sensational side dish to a bigger meal.

I normally cook green vegetables for a few minute tops, to retain their vibrant green colour and crunch, but this is one notable exception. After 20–25 minutes of slowly simmering in a simple tomato, garlic and herb sauce, the flat beans still have a mouthwatering texture, and the flavour is out of this world.

3 tablespoons extra-virgin olive oil
2 garlic cloves, finely chopped
400 g can chopped tomatoes
salt flakes
600 g Italian flat beans, trimmed
    and cut in half
crusty bread, to serve

Heat the olive oil in a medium-sized skillet over medium–low heat, add the garlic and let it sizzle for 30 seconds or until pale golden. Add the tomatoes and a little salt and stir well. Add the beans, then cover with a lid and simmer for 20–25 minutes or until soft.

Taste for seasoning and adjust accordingly, then serve with some crusty bread for mopping up the sauce.

BRUSCHETTA CON FAGIOLI AL FORNO E CAPRINO

(GOAT'S CHEESE BRUSCHETTA WITH BRAISED BEANS AND TOMATOES)

SERVES 4–6

Think Italian-style baked beans with all the accoutrements we love, such as tomatoes, chillies and creamy goat's cheese. And the best part is that for this recipe you don't even have to go to the trouble of soaking beans overnight and boiling them before using them, as canned ones are perfect for this timeless recipe, which bears similarities with the ancient Tuscan classic fagioli all'uccelletto.

Preheat your oven to 180°C. Line a large deep baking tray with baking paper.

Combine the beans, tomato halves, chilli, garlic, wine, olive oil, rosemary and cheese rind in a large bowl, season with salt and pepper and mix well. Tumble onto the tray and bake, turning the garlic halves over once (so they bake cut-side down and then cut-side up), for 35–40 minutes or until the tomatoes are slightly scorched and the garlic is very soft. Remove the garlic and transfer the braised bean mixture and juices to a serving bowl.

Squeeze out a few garlic cloves, mash them with a fork, then add them to the bowl and mix well. Add the juices that have collected on the tray. Squeeze out a few more garlic cloves (use as many as you like) and spread them on the baguette slices. Top with some goat's cheese and salt and pepper and serve with the braised beans and tomatoes.

400 g can borlotti beans, well drained

400 g can cannellini beans, well drained

600 g mixed cherry tomatoes, cut in half

2–3 small red chillies, cut in half lengthways

1 head of garlic, cut in half horizontally

100 ml dry white wine

2½ tablespoons extra-virgin olive oil

a few rosemary sprigs

small piece of parmigiano or pecorino rind

salt flakes and freshly ground black pepper

1 baguette, thinly sliced and toasted

200 g soft goat's cheese

109

ZUPPA DI COZZE E FAGIOLI PICCANTE

(SPICY MUSSEL AND BORLOTTI BEAN STEW)

SERVES 4

The combination of legumes and seafood is a favourite with Italian home cooks, combining salty, creamy and nutty characteristics into a stunning marriage of flavours. Chickpeas seem to love the sapidity of vongole and the sweetness of prawns and scampi, while the faint mushroom undertones of mussels are more likely to be paired with earthy borlotti beans, as in this stunning seafood zuppa (stew).

Because of the simplicity of this dish, I suggest using dried borlotti beans but, if you can get your hands on them, by all means use freshly podded ones.

You'll need to start this recipe a day ahead.

If you are using dried borlotti beans, soak them in plenty of water overnight. Drain and rinse well, then place them in a saucepan and cover with water. Add the bay leaf and cook, topping up with water if needed, over medium heat for 45–60 minutes or until tender. Don't add any salt at this stage or they will crack. Set aside to cool in their liquid. Alternatively, if you are using fresh borlotti beans, boil them for 35–40 minutes then drain and set aside.

Heat the olive oil in a large heavy-based saucepan over medium heat. Add the spring onion, chilli and garlic and cook for 1–2 minutes or until fragrant. Pour in the wine and allow it to bubble away for 2–3 minutes to cook out the alcohol. Add the mussels, tomato and 200 ml of water, cover with a lid and cook for 4–5 minutes or until the mussels have opened. Taste for salt and adjust to your liking. Add the borlotti beans and season with more salt, if needed, and pepper.

Thinly slice the reserved dark-green parts of the spring onion, then divide the stew among bowls, top with the spring onion and serve with chilli oil and lots of crusty bread.

NOTE

When you buy mussels, they are most likely already scrubbed clean, however, they will still have a fluffy beard attached to the shell, which you can remove by simply tugging on it with conviction.

---

200 g (1 cup) dried borlotti beans (or 2 cups podded fresh borlotti beans)

1 bay leaf

3 tablespoons extra-virgin olive oil

1–2 spring onions, white and pale green parts thinly sliced, dark-green parts reserved

1–2 bird's eye chillies, thinly sliced

2 garlic cloves, crushed

150 ml dry white wine

1 kg mussels, scrubbed and debearded (see Note)

250 g vine-ripened tomatoes, chopped

salt flakes and freshly ground black pepper

TO SERVE

chilli oil

crusty bread

RIBOLLITA TOSCANA
(TUSCAN TWICE-COOKED SOUP WITH BEANS AND CAVOLO NERO)

SERVES 4

This combination of nutty beans, chunks of rustic bread and sturdy cavolo nero has no rival when it comes to hearty peasant food. The name ribollita means twice cooked, and indeed you are required to first stew your cooked beans in a rich tomato stock. Stale bread is added to absorb the liquid and thicken the sauce, then it is dusted with cheese and baked until golden.

To make the stock, pour water into a large saucepan until it's three-quarters full. Add the beans, potato, tomato, bay leaf, onion and pancetta or speck. Don't add any salt at this stage, as it will cause the beans to wrinkle. Cook over medium–low heat for 1 hour or until the beans are tender. Skim off any foam that comes to the surface. Remove from the heat and stir in a couple of teaspoons of salt and some pepper. Set aside.

Heat the olive oil in a large flameproof casserole dish over medium–low heat. Add the vegetables, chopped garlic and a little salt and cook for 10 minutes or until the vegetables are softened, but not browned. Stir in the tomatoes.

Using a slotted spoon, remove the beans from the stock (discard the bay leaf, vegetables and pancetta). Add the beans to the dish, along with 400 ml of the stock. Add the cheese rind and bring to a simmer. Stir in the cavolo nero and cook over medium–low heat for 10 minutes or until the greens are tender and the liquid has reduced slightly. Discard the cheese rind.

Preheat your oven to 220°C.

Rub the slices of bread with the cut side of the remaining garlic clove, then dip them into the bean mixture, so they are half submerged and half sticking out, to allow the edges to crisp up. Taste for salt and pepper and adjust. Generously dust pecorino over top, then bake for 25–30 minutes or until the bread has absorbed most of the liquid and the top is golden and crusty. Drizzle with some extra olive oil and enjoy hot or warm.

NOTES

I never throw away my parmigiano or pecorino rinds, even when there is seemingly nothing left to grate. Simmered in a stock or soup, the cheese that can't be grated will melt off the rind, giving your dish a richer flavour.

You can also use freshly podded borlotti beans instead of dried. They will take about 35–40 minutes to cook.

---

3 tablespoons extra-virgin olive oil, plus extra for drizzling

1 onion, roughly chopped

1 carrot, roughly chopped

1 celery stalk, roughly chopped

2 garlic cloves, 1 roughly chopped, the other peeled and cut in half

200 g canned peeled or chopped tomatoes

small piece of parmigiano rind (see Notes)

1 bunch of cavolo nero, well washed, stalks removed, leaves roughly chopped

8 thick slices of sourdough

freshly grated pecorino, for dusting

STOCK

400 g (2 cups) dried cannellini or borlotti beans, soaked overnight and drained (see Notes)

1 potato, peeled

1 tomato

1 bay leaf

1 small onion, peeled

30 g piece of smoked pancetta or speck

salt flakes and freshly ground black pepper

FAVE E CICORIA
(FAVA BEAN PUREE WITH SAUTEED CHICORY)

SERVES 4

This unassuming four-ingredient meal, one of the signature dishes of Puglia, consists of a creamy puree of fava beans (dried broad beans) topped with chicory sauteed in olive oil. And that's it! Italian simplicity on a plate.

You'll need to start this recipe a day ahead.

Place your fava beans in a large saucepan and add enough water to fully submerge them. Season well with salt and pepper and bring to a simmer over medium–low heat. Simmer, stirring frequently and adding more water as needed to prevent them from drying out, for 1 hour or until the fava beans are very tender and the water has been absorbed. Stir vigorously with a wooden spoon to give them a creamy texture. If you prefer a smoother consistency, whiz them with a stick blender. (I like some chunky bits!) Drizzle over 2–3 tablespoons of the olive oil, season to taste and set aside.

To prepare the chicory, trim off the white base and discard any bruised leaves. Place the chicory in a large saucepan of boiling salted water for about 1–2 minutes, then drain and immediately plunge into ice-cold water to preserve its vibrant colour. Drain again.

Heat the remaining oil in a large heavy-based frying pan over medium–high heat, add the garlic and cook for 1 minute or until fragrant. Add the chicory and saute for 2–3 minutes or until wilted. Discard the garlic. Season the chicory with salt.

Spoon the fava bean puree into serving bowls, top with the chicory and oil from the pan and drizzle over a little extra oil, if you like. Enjoy!

NOTE

If dried fava beans are hard to come by, or if you crave this dish but don't have 24 hours soaking time to spare, you can use 2 x 400 g cans of chickpeas instead. Simply drain them and whiz in the food processor like you would for the fava beans. They have a very similar flavour profile and nutritional value, but will be ready in no time at all!

300 g dried fava beans (dried broad beans), soaked overnight in plenty of water, drained

salt flakes and freshly ground black pepper

75 ml extra-virgin olive oil, plus extra for drizzling (optional)

1 large bunch of chicory

1–2 garlic cloves, skin on, bashed with the back of a knife

INSALATA DI ORZO E FUNGHI TRIFOLATI

(PEARL BARLEY AND PAN-ROASTED MUSHROOM SALAD)

SERVES 4

The natural earthy flavour of barley is matched to perfection by the warmth of mushrooms pan-roasted with that holy trinity of ingredients: garlic, butter and parsley. If fresh truffles are in season, skip the almonds and crown instead with dark shavings of this extravagant, knobbly bulb to elevate this autumnal salad to a higher level ...

Bring a saucepan of salted water to the boil, add the pearl barley and cook for 30–35 minutes or until al dente. Drain and set aside.

While the barley is cooking, heat the butter and 1 tablespoon of the olive oil in a large heavy-based frying pan over high heat. Add the chopped parsley stalks and mushroom, then season with salt and pepper and stir. Add the garlic and cook for 45–60 seconds. Turn the heat to low, cover with a lid and cook, stirring occasionally, for 10–12 minutes or until the mushroom is soft. Taste for salt and adjust to your liking, then add 1 tablespoon of the vinegar and stir well.

Season the cooked barley with the remaining olive oil and vinegar, and add salt and pepper as needed. Mix the barley into the mushroom, tumble onto a serving platter and scatter the parsley leaves and flaked almonds over the top.

200 g pearl barley

40 g butter

3 tablespoons extra-virgin olive oil

1 tablespoon finely chopped flat-leaf parsley stalks

500 g mixed mushrooms (such as field, portobello or brown), scrubbed and sliced

salt flakes and freshly ground black pepper

2 garlic cloves, crushed

3 tablespoons white balsamic vinegar or apple cider vinegar

2 tablespoons roughly chopped flat-leaf parsley leaves

3 tablespoons flaked almonds, toasted

ORZO RISOTTATO CON PISELLINI E GAMBERI
(BARLEY RISOTTO WITH PEA PESTO AND PRAWNS)

SERVES 4

3 tablespoons extra-virgin olive oil

2 golden shallots, thinly sliced

330 g (1½ cups) pearl barley

150 ml dry white wine

1.5 litres vegetable or chicken stock,
    brought to a gentle simmer,
    plus extra for the pesto

40 g butter

12 raw banana prawns, peeled
    and deveined, tails left intact

basil leaves or pea tendrils, to serve

finely grated lemon zest, to serve

PEA PESTO

155 g (1 cup) frozen or freshly shelled
    peas, cooked in salted boiling
    water for 5 minutes

3 tablespoons extra-virgin olive oil

1 small bunch of basil leaves

65 g (⅔ cup) freshly grated
    parmigiano

salt flakes and freshly ground
    black pepper

juice of ½ lemon

Using barley in a risotto is a creative way to turn this earthy grain into a more sophisticated food offering. The method is the same as if using rice (but remember that, unlike rice, barley contains gluten), and very much as with a traditional risotto recipe, the secret to a stunning, creamy texture is in those final moments, when, off the heat, you add butter and parmigiano and stir like life on planet Earth depends on it. This process is called 'mantecatura' and it is the key to creating that elusive 'all'onda' (like waves) consistency. Set aside a little extra time when making your barley risotto as the grain will take about 35 minutes to reach al dente perfection.

Heat the olive oil in a large heavy-based frying pan over medium heat, add the shallot and stir-fry for 1–2 minutes or until fragrant. Add the pearl barley and stir to coat well in the oil and shallot. Pour in the wine and allow it to bubble away for 2–3 minutes or until the alcohol has evaporated. Turn the heat to low, ladle in enough stock to cover the barley, then stir gently. Continue to add the stock as it gets absorbed, giving the occasional gentle stir, for 30–35 minutes or until the barley is cooked through but still slightly al dente. Add the butter and stir vigorously for 30 seconds. Add the prawns, cover with a lid and turn off the heat. Allow the residual heat to just cook the prawns.

Meanwhile, to make the pea pesto, combine the cooked peas and a couple of tablespoons of stock in a food processor. Add the olive oil, basil, parmigiano and salt and pepper and whiz to combine. Add the lemon juice, adjust the seasoning and set aside.

To serve, ladle the barley and prawn risotto into shallow bowls, swirl through a couple of tablespoons of pea pesto and top with some basil leaves or pea tendrils and lemon zest.

NOTES

Store any leftover pea pesto, covered in olive oil and in an airtight container, in the fridge for up to 1 week.

MINESTRONE CON FARRO
(FARRO AND VEGETABLE SOUP)

SERVES 4

3 tablespoons extra-virgin olive oil,
  plus extra to serve
1 leek, well washed and thinly sliced
1 small carrot, sliced
1 celery stalk, sliced
1 small red chilli, thinly sliced
1 garlic clove, finely chopped
1 small handful of diced pancetta
  or speck (optional: omit for a
  vegan version)
170 g (¾ cup) farro
160 g (⅔ cup) canned peeled or
  chopped tomatoes
2 litres chicken or vegetable stock
  or water
2 red potatoes, cut into 2 cm cubes
125 g green beans (or flat beans),
  topped and tailed and cut into
  chunks
80 g (½ cup) frozen peas
salt flakes and freshly ground
  black pepper
finely grated zest of ½ lemon
baby basil and mint leaves, to serve

Minestrone is the augmented word for minestra (soup); the 'one' suffix turns a humble soup into a more robust one. The upgrade is generally given by adding greens, potatoes, pancetta and grains to a simple vegetable broth. What the 'one' at the end of the word does to me, particularly, is paint my face with a huge smile as I am a devout lover of any simple meal that can be pimped up into a more substantial one. Perfect for cold nights in with a glass of red and a plush blanket.

Heat the olive oil in a large heavy-based saucepan over medium heat, add the leek, carrot, celery and chilli and saute for 2–3 minutes or until softened. Stir in the garlic and pancetta or speck (if using) and cook, allowing the flavours to mingle, for 2–3 minutes.

Add the farro, tomatoes and stock or water to the pan – the vegetables and farro should be completely submerged, so add a little more if necessary. Bring to the boil, then reduce the heat to low and simmer for 20 minutes. Stir in the potato and cook for a further 10 minutes. Add the beans and peas and cook for 5 minutes or until the farro is al dente.

Season with salt and pepper. Serve hot with a good swirl of extra olive oil and the lemon zest and basil and mint leaves scattered over the top.

FRITTELLE DI FARRO E ZUCCHINE

(SPELT AND ZUCCHINI FRITTERS)

SERVES 4

Like many other grains, spelt is harvested for flour production and can pretty much be used in place of regular white flour with no significant alteration to recipes. When used in these savoury frittelle (fritters), it mainly acts as the glue to hold the zucchini together, offering a thoroughly satisfying mouthful, as well as a subdued nutty flavour. If you can find wholemeal spelt flour, then don't think twice about using it, just be sure to add an extra 2½ tablespoons of water to the batter.

Place the zucchini in a bowl and season with salt. Stand for 10 minutes, then wrap the zucchini in a clean tea towel and squeeze out all the excess moisture. This will result in a better fritter that won't get soggy.

Combine the flour and baking powder in a large bowl. Add the egg and 100 ml of water, mix well, then add the spring onion, lemon zest and grated parmigiano. Season with salt and pepper, then add the grated zucchini and toss to combine.

Heat the olive oil in a large heavy-based frying pan over medium–high heat, then drop in 2 tablespoons of batter for each fritter and cook 3–4 fritters at a time (you don't want to overcrowd the pan). Cook for 2–3 minutes or until the underside is golden. Turn the fritters and fry on the other side until browned. Drain on paper towel as you continue to fry the rest.

Serve with the extra lemon zest, a chunk of parmigiano and slices of prosciutto, if desired, or anything else that takes your fancy.

2 zucchini, coarsely grated or julienned
salt flakes and freshly ground black pepper
200 g spelt flour
1 scant tablespoon baking powder
2 large eggs, lightly beaten
1 spring onion, thinly sliced
finely grated zest of 1 lemon, plus extra to serve
2 tablespoons freshly grated parmigiano
100 ml olive oil
chunk of parmigiano and slices of prosciutto, to serve (optional)

SFORMATO DI BROCCOLI, SALSICCIA E POLENTA

(POLENTA, SAUSAGE AND BROCCOLI BAKE)

SERVES 4–6

This simple polenta bake encapsulates the principles of cucina povera (peasant cooking), where a few unassuming ingredients are combined to fulfil their greater potential in an incredibly cost-effective way. This dish also happens to be gluten free – how virtuous.

Heat the olive oil in a large heavy-based frying pan over medium–high heat, add the pork and chilli and saute, stirring occasionally, for 3–4 minutes or until the pork is browned. Deglaze the pan with the wine, scraping up any bits caught on the base, and allow it to bubble away for 2–3 minutes or until the alcohol has evaporated. Turn the heat to low and cook for a further 10–15 minutes or until the pork is cooked through. Season with salt and pepper to taste and set aside.

Blanch the broccoli in salted boiling water for 5 minutes or until tender. Drain and rinse under cold water to preserve its vibrant colour. Add to the pork mixture and stir through. Taste for salt and adjust accordingly, then set aside.

Preheat your oven to 200°C. Grease a 20 cm pie dish with oil and dust with the extra polenta.

Place 800 ml of water and the polenta in a non-stick saucepan, add a good pinch of salt and bring to a simmer. Cook gently, stirring occasionally, for 2–3 minutes or until the polenta is soft and creamy. Remove from the heat, stir in the parmigiano and set aside.

Spread half of the cooked polenta in the dish to create a base. Add the pork mixture, spreading it out evenly. Top with the remaining polenta to create a lid. Bake for 20 minutes or until lovely and golden. Serve with a green salad as a main course.

3–4 tablespoons extra-virgin olive oil, plus extra for greasing

300 g pork sausage meat squeezed from its casing, cut into small pieces

1 small red chilli, finely chopped

100 ml dry white wine

salt flakes and freshly ground black pepper

1 head of broccoli, cut into florets

250 g instant polenta, plus extra for dusting

3 tablespoons freshly grated parmigiano

green salad, to serve

EGGS

N°. 3
EGGS & DAIRY

DAIRY

Eggs and dairy occupy a special place in the kitchen – and heart – of the Italian home cook.

On those days when both fridge and pantry seem desolate and empty, if there are eggs in the fridge, there's a meal. Italians love these self-contained powerhouses for their nutritional value, as well as their versatility. Feeling under the weather? Mamma or nonna will whip up a delicious bowl of minestra stracciatella (egg-drop soup, see page 137). Need a nutritious meal in under 30 minutes? Uova alla contadina (eggs poached in tomato sugo, see page 130) is the answer. Got leftover spaghetti? Go all Neapolitan and give them a new 'frittata' look (see page 140).

The same devotion is reserved for dairy. Whether it is milk – artfully frothed to crown your morning coffee – or cheese, dairy never goes amiss in the vast repertoire of Italian home cooking. We turn to ricotta for sweet and savoury preparations, we don't spend a single day separated from parmigiano, cut into chunks and added to an antipasto board, or grated over our favourite pasta dish. Such is our love for it, we don't even part with the rind, which is always added to soups for that extra savoury touch.

While one should not have a favourite, if you were to try any recipe from this chapter, I urge you to give my uova ripiene (devilled eggs, see page 138) a go. They were indeed a favourite of the crew on the day we shot these recipes, and my teenage son and his friends scoffed up the leftovers in a matter of seconds. If you are looking for a science project to engage curious kids, I've included recipes for homemade cheese curd (see page 142) – very similar to ricotta and just as versatile – and luscious mascarpone (see page 155).

UOVA ALLA CONTADINA
(EGGS POACHED IN TOMATO SUGO)

SERVES 4

This is one of the signature dishes of Nonna Irene (my mum's mamma). She would always make a large batch of sugo for Sunday pasta, and the leftover sauce was the perfect poaching liquid for eggs. The name 'alla contadina' means farmers' style, an expression used in many no-fuss recipes in the Italian home-cooking repertoire. Clearly, contadini don't have time to indulge in elaborate courses – they need something fast, nutritious and delicious, and this Italian-style shakshuka fits the bill perfectly.

Heat the olive oil in a wide saucepan over medium heat. Add the shallot, celery, 'nduja and capsicum and cook, stirring occasionally, for 2–3 minutes or until the shallot is softened and golden.

Add the tomatoes, cheese rind and 200 ml of water to the pan and bring to the boil. Reduce the heat to low and simmer gently for 15–20 minutes or until slightly reduced. (You can either discard the piece of capsicum or leave it in – it is simply there to impart extra flavour.)

Make four indentations in the sugo with the back of a spoon. Crack the eggs, one by one, into the indentations and cook for 6–8 minutes – just enough to set the whites but keep the yolks runny, or cook for longer if you prefer your eggs more set. (You will notice that eggs poached in a sauce take a bit longer than poaching in water.)

Remove from the heat, season with salt to taste and dust with some grated parmigiano, if you like. Top with a few celery leaves, drizzle with chilli oil and serve with plenty of crusty bread.

NOTE
'Nduja is a spicy salami, chilli and garlic paste typical of Calabria, in Italy's south. It is often used as a flavouring in stews and sauces or even spread on toasted bread.

3 tablespoons extra-virgin olive oil
2 golden shallots, finely chopped
1 small celery stalk, thinly sliced
1 teaspoon 'nduja (see Note)
¼ red capsicum, deseeded
400 g can crushed tomatoes
    (or passata)
1 small piece of parmigiano rind
4 eggs

TO SERVE
salt flakes
freshly grated parmigiano (optional)
celery leaves
chilli oil
crusty bread

TORTA PASQUALINA
(EGG, RICOTTA AND SPINACH PIE)

SERVES 6–8

This savoury pie is traditionally made for Easter ('Pasqua' in Italian), but can be enjoyed all year round so long as you have bitter green leaves on hand. Spinach can be replaced with silverbeet or even cavolo nero – the only rule to live by is to squeeze all the moisture out of the cooked greens to safeguard the crunch of the pastry. Other than that, you can really unleash your culinary creativity and add smoked speck or pancetta and, if you have nimble hands, enclose the filling with intricate lattice patterns.

Preheat your oven to 200°C. Line a 24 cm round springform cake tin with baking paper.

To make the pastry, place the flour and olive oil in a bowl, add 200 ml of water and mix well. Tip the dough onto a floured surface and knead for a few minutes until it comes together to form a smooth ball. Cover with a tea towel or beeswax wrap and rest at room temperature for 20 minutes.

In the meantime, heat the olive oil in a large heavy-based frying pan over high heat. Add the garlic and cook for 30 seconds or until fragrant. Add the spinach and cover with a lid. Cook for 2–3 minutes or until just wilted. Season with salt to taste and leave to cool slightly. Remove the garlic and discard, then drain the spinach in a colander, pressing down to remove the excess liquid.

Combine the spinach, ricotta, nutmeg, lemon zest, cheeses and two of the eggs in a large bowl, season with salt and pepper and set aside.

Divide the dough into two portions, one slightly larger than the other. Roll out the larger portion on a lightly floured surface until 5 mm thick, then use it to line the base of the tin, making sure the dough hangs about 5 cm over the rim of the tin to create a pastry case. Spoon the spinach and ricotta filling into the pastry case, then smooth out the surface.

Roll out the remaining piece of dough until 5 mm thick and cut into six long strips. Take three of the pastry strips and plait them together, then repeat to make a second plait. Crack four of the remaining eggs on top of the filling, then fold the overhanging pastry over the eggs and filling. Arrange the plaits on top to form a cross, then beat the remaining egg and brush it over the pastry. Transfer the pie to a baking tray and bake for 40–45 minutes or until the top is golden and the eggs are cooked.

2 tablespoons extra-virgin olive oil

1 garlic clove, skin on, bashed with the back of a knife

500 g baby spinach leaves

salt flakes and freshly ground black pepper

400 g fresh ricotta, drained

1 teaspoon freshly ground nutmeg

finely grated zest of ½ lemon

50 g (½ cup) freshly grated parmigiano

45 g (½ cup) freshly grated pecorino

7 eggs

PASTRY

400 g (2⅔ cups) type 00 flour, plus extra for dusting

3 tablespoons extra-virgin olive oil

MINESTRA STRACCIATELLA
(EGG-DROP SOUP)

SERVES 4

Some dishes have the unique power to provide a sense of nurture as well as nutrition. It is certainly the case with minestra stracciatella, a classic egg-drop soup from the Emilia-Romagna region, where hot stock, generally leftover from other preparations, is repurposed and given a little lift with the addition of barely cooked strips of egg flavoured with cheese and nutmeg. Think of this as a cuddle in soup form.

The name stracciatella comes from the word 'stracci', meaning rags, which is more or less the way the egg mixture looks once it is whisked through the hot stock. This is the kind of recipe that showcases the resourcefulness and creativity of Italian home cooks. Humble and divine.

4 eggs

75 g freshly grated pecorino

¼ teaspoon freshly ground nutmeg

1 tablespoon finely chopped
   flat-leaf parsley leaves

salt flakes and freshly ground
   black pepper

2 litres chicken, beef or vegetable
   stock

crusty bread, to serve (optional)

Beat the eggs in a large bowl. Add the cheese, nutmeg, parsley and a little salt and pepper (keeping in mind that the pecorino is already very flavourful).

Pour the stock into a large saucepan and bring to a gentle simmer, then slowly pour in the egg mixture, stirring with a whisk. As the egg mixture touches the hot stock, it will start to cook and separate into strips. Cook for 2–3 minutes, then serve in bowls with lots of crusty bread, if desired.

UOVA RIPIENE CON TONNO E MASCARPONE
(DEVILLED EGGS <u>WITH</u> TUNA <u>AND</u> MASCARPONE)

MAKES 12

Here's a fun retro recipe to try. Uova ripiene (devilled eggs) were all the rage in the 1980s when I was growing up in Italy. It is fair to say I have not enjoyed them many times since, but the recipe has been caught in its own time warp for far too long. It's time to revive it – and dust off the piping bag that I never seem to get to play with.

To hard-boil the eggs, lower them gently into a large saucepan of simmering water, bring to the boil and cook for 8–9 minutes. Rinse under cold water to stop them cooking further and leave to cool.

Peel the eggs and cut them in half lengthways. Scoop out the yolks, place them in a bowl and mash well with a fork. Add the mascarpone, tuna, mustard and chives. Season with salt and pepper to taste and mix to a smooth paste.

Fill a piping bag with the egg-yolk mixture, then choose your preferred nozzle. Pipe the egg-yolk mixture into the egg-white cavities. Alternatively, you can fill each egg-white cavity with teaspoonfuls of the egg-yolk mixture. Top with the extra chives and serve.

6 eggs

70 g mascarpone

80 g canned tuna in brine,
  well drained

1 teaspoon dijon mustard

1 tablespoon finely chopped chives,
  plus extra to serve

salt flakes and freshly ground
  black pepper

FRITTATA DI SPAGHETTI
(LEFTOVER SPAGHETTI FRITTATA)

SERVES 4–6

The name of this recipe gives away the cooking method and the sentiment behind it: re-use leftover spaghetti, throw in a few beaten eggs and some seasoning and transform it into a delicious, golden frittata. Think of it as the Neapolitan bubble and squeak!

One would assume that Italians would pay the same courtesy to any leftover pasta shape; however, the likes of penne, fusilli or rigatoni tend to be more easily turned into pasta bakes, making spaghetti the pasta of choice for the savvy Neapolitan home cooks we owe this recipe to.

This dish honours tradition and the fundamental Italian home-cooking principle of not wasting food. Leftovers are given new life and often become even more intriguing than the original recipe. Frittata di spaghetti is excellent warm or at room temperature. Don't be scared to take that burnt golden crunch as far as it can go ... your palate will thank you for it.

Mix the egg, cheese, milk and some salt and pepper in a large bowl. Add the leftover spaghetti and combine.

Heat 2 tablespoons of the olive oil in a 20 cm non-stick frying pan over medium–high heat. Tip in the spaghetti and egg mixture and swirl it around to cover the base of the pan. Cook for 3–4 minutes or until you can see the underside is turning golden brown. Slide the frittata onto a plate.

Add the remaining oil to the pan and allow it to get hot. With one swift and confident movement, tip the frittata upside down into the pan so that the golden bottom is now on top. Cook for 2–3 minutes, then slide onto a serving plate.

Dust a little extra grated parmigiano over the top, if you like, then cut into wedges and serve. This is excellent freshly prepared or served cold.

6 eggs, beaten

35 g (⅓ cup) freshly grated parmigiano, plus extra to serve (optional)

100 ml milk

salt flakes and freshly ground black pepper

300 g cold leftover spaghetti (in any kind of sauce – tomato, ragu, puttanesca, carbonara are all fine!)

80 ml (⅓ cup) extra-virgin olive oil

CAGLIATA CON UVA ARROSTO E CROSTINI

(HOMEMADE CHEESE CURD <u>WITH</u> ROASTED GRAPES <u>AND</u> CROSTINI)

SERVES 6–8

If you have milk and lemon, then you have homemade cheese. It really is as easy as that. It's incredibly satisfying to watch milk separate from its whey and set into soft curds. Once squeezed between layers of muslin, the curds can be enjoyed in their softer form, or left to set and then sliced. The leftover whey is a precious nectar that must not be discarded. It can be used in place of buttermilk in baking, or reheated and turned into ricotta, which translates as 'twice cooked'. All this from milk and a few drops of lemon juice!

To make the cheese curd, pour the milk and cream into a large saucepan and bring to just below simmering point (around 90°C). Add the lemon juice and a pinch of salt, stir and turn off the heat. Cover with a lid and leave for 10 minutes to allow the curds to form.

Line a large bowl with a double layer of muslin cloth. Use a slotted spoon to scoop up the curds and tip them into the bowl. Lift the corners of the cloth and tie them into a knot, then slide a wooden spoon handle under the knot to suspend the bundle over the bowl. Set aside to drain for 30 minutes, then scoop the curd into a bowl. Pour the whey into a jar, cover and refrigerate for up to 2 days (see Note on page 155 for ideas on how to use the whey).

Preheat your oven to 200°C. Line a baking tray with baking paper.

Place the grapes in a large bowl and crush some with your hands to release their juices, keeping the rest whole. Add the olive oil, vincotto, rosemary and some salt and pepper, mix and tumble onto the tray. Roast for 25 minutes or until the grapes are scorched.

Toast the baguette slices until crisp. Spread some curd on the toasted bread, top with the grapes, drizzle on the roasting juices and enjoy.

NOTES

Vincotto is a syrupy condiment made from grape must and is easily available in well-stocked supermarkets; balsamic vinegar is a great alternative.

Store any leftover curd in an airtight container in the fridge for up to 3 days. It will firm up as it sets.

---

180 g (1 cup) seedless red grapes
180 g (1 cup) seedless white grapes
2 tablespoons extra-virgin olive oil
2 tablespoons vincotto (see Notes)
a few rosemary sprigs
freshly ground black pepper
1 baguette, thinly sliced

CHEESE CURD (MAKES 250 G)
2 litres full-cream milk
150 ml double cream
juice of 1 large lemon
salt flakes

143

FIADONCINI ABRUZZESI
(RUSTIC CHEESE PARCELS FROM ABRUZZO)

MAKES ABOUT 20

Abruzzo is the beautiful region in central–southern Italy where my mum comes from, and I proudly declare myself half Milanese, half Abruzzese at any opportunity. My Abruzzese half embraces the unassuming beauty of peasant-style cuisine, where the ingredients are never overcomplicated. Recipes are traditional and passed on from family to family with pride and a sense of legacy, and in that same spirit I would never try to alter any of them for the sake of modernising a dish.

Fiadoncini are nothing more than rustic parcels of a simple parmigiano and pecorino filling enclosed in an olive oil and white wine pastry. I feel nothing but love and gratitude for those who have passed this recipe on to us. And so, we pay it forward and carry on this legacy, knowing that somewhere, someone is willing to roll out thin sheets of pastry to accommodate a taste of Abruzzo.

You will notice that the ingredients list uses a tumbler as a measuring cup. I have left it there as a tribute to the way cooking is approached in Italy: 'un bicchiere di vino bianco, mezzo bicchiere d'olio e la farina che prende' (a bit of this, a bit of that and flour as needed to create a dough). Having migrated to Australia, I do miss Abruzzo so much, yet making the food of my mum's homeland lessens the heartache a little.

To make the olive oil pastry, place the flour in a large bowl, add the eggs, wine, olive oil and a pinch of salt and mix until combined. If the dough feels too dry, add a little water. Tip the dough onto a floured surface and knead for 5–10 minutes or until it comes together to form a smooth ball. Cover with a tea towel or beeswax wrap and rest at room temperature for 10 minutes.

Meanwhile, place the cheese, eggs and a little salt and pepper in a large bowl and mix well.

600 g mixed freshly grated parmigiano and sharp pecorino
6 eggs
freshly ground black pepper

OLIVE OIL PASTRY
700 g type 00 or plain flour, plus extra for dusting
2 eggs
1 tumbler of white wine (about 200 ml)
½ tumbler of extra-virgin olive oil (about 100 ml)
salt flakes

>

Preheat your oven to 180°C. Line two large baking trays with baking paper.

Once your dough has rested, use a rolling pin and a floured surface, a pasta machine or simply your hands to roll or stretch it out until it is 2–3 mm thick.

To make the fiadoncini, cut the rolled dough into 30 cm × 15 cm sheets and, working with one sheet at a time (cover the other sheets with a damp tea towel), lay out flat on a floured surface. Starting at one end of the sheet, dollop 1 tablespoon of the egg and cheese mixture in the middle, then continue at 3 cm intervals until you get to the other end. Brush around the filling with water to moisten, then fold the sheet over (as if making ravioli) and press down to seal. Gently press around each mound to remove any air bubbles. Use a fluted cutter to cut into half-moon shapes, score the top once with a sharp knife and place on the trays. Repeat with the remaining sheets of dough and filling.

Bake for 20 minutes or until golden, puffed and cooked through. Serve warm or at room temperature.

CASATIELLO
(NEAPOLITAN EASTER PIE)

SERVES 8–10

Casatiello passionately belongs in a chapter dedicated to eggs and dairy as the bread shell contains an extraordinarily rich cheese filling, and whole eggs – representing the Easter symbols of rebirth and fertility – crown the pie. Because of the heftiness of this dish, a thin slice goes a long way, making casatiello perfect for picnics. It is traditionally served in Italy during 'le scampagnate del Lunedì dell'Angelo' (Easter Monday outdoor gatherings).

Start by making the pastry. Combine the yeast and lukewarm water in a small bowl and mix. Place the flour in the bowl of an electric mixer fitted with the dough hook, add the yeasted water, olive oil and butter. Add salt and pepper to your liking, then knead for a couple of minutes on low speed to combine the ingredients. Increase the speed a little and knead for a further 2 minutes or until the dough is smooth. If the dough is too sticky, add a little extra flour.

Shape the dough into a ball, place in a large lightly oiled bowl, cover with a damp tea towel and set aside to rise at room temperature for 1–2 hours or until doubled in volume. If you are in a warmer climate, this won't take quite as long.

Lift the dough out of the bowl with floured hands and place on a floured surface. Cut off one-eighth of the dough, cover and set aside for later (you will need this to create the crosses to hold the eggs in place). Stretch the remaining dough out to form a 1 cm thick rectangle. Distribute the salami, mortadella, provolone and asiago over the dough, leaving a 2 cm border around the edges. Dust with the pecorino and parmigiano, then roll the dough up along the long side into a sausage shape.

Grease a non-stick bundt tin with olive oil or butter. Transfer the pastry roll, seam-side down, to the tin. Place the four washed eggs on top of the pastry, pressing them on gently.

100 g salami, cut into small cubes

100 g mortadella, cut into small cubes

100 g provolone, cut into small cubes

100 g asiago, cut into small cubes

25 g (¼ cup) freshly grated pecorino

25 g (¼ cup) freshly grated parmigiano

4 small eggs, well washed (they sit in their shells on the uncooked pastry)

PASTRY

7 g sachet dried yeast

250 ml (1 cup) lukewarm water

500 g (3⅓ cups) type oo flour, plus extra if needed and for dusting

75 ml olive oil

30 g butter, softened

salt flakes and freshly ground black pepper

EGG WASH

1 egg

2 tablespoons milk

Roll out the reserved dough, dusting with flour if needed, until 5 mm thick. Cut into eight 10 cm × 1 cm strips. Use two strips of pastry to create a cross pattern on top of each egg. Cover with a damp tea towel and allow to prove at room temperature for 2 hours or until the dough is puffy and has almost filled the tin.

When almost ready to cook, preheat your oven to 180°C.

To make the egg wash, lightly beat the egg and milk in a small bowl. Brush the pastry with the egg wash, then bake the pie for 50–60 minutes or until it is golden brown on top and the bottom is cooked through.

Cool in the tin for 10 minutes, then gently remove the pie and cool on a wire rack for 30–45 minutes before serving either warm or at room temperature. Traditionally, we remove the cooked eggs from the pastry after baking, peel and slice them, and enjoy them with a slice of casatiello.

RUSTICI LECCESI
(PUGLIESE CHEESE BITES)

MAKES 8

These mouthwatering parcels come with a warning: don't eat them straight out of the oven! The cheesy besciamella (white sauce) within the crunchy shell is lava hot and, while tempting, a bite will scald your mouth mercilessly. If you are patient enough, these delightful bites are sensational warm or at room temperature, their creamy filling creating the perfect juxtaposition to the golden, crispy pastry shields.

The filling can be customised to your liking: you can replace the pancetta with ham or even anchovies, and you can add a little chopped tomato, too. You may want to double the recipe if you are hosting drinks and nibbles . . . they will disappear as soon as they hit the table.

To make the besciamella, fry the pancetta in the olive oil in a small frying pan over medium heat for 2–3 minutes or until slightly caramelised, then set aside to cool. While the pancetta is cooling, melt the butter with the flour in a small saucepan over medium heat, stirring constantly. The mixture will solidify into a wet sand texture – at this point, slowly start pouring in the milk, a little at a time, whisking well to avoid lumps. Turn the heat to low and continue cooking and stirring with a wooden spoon until the mixture starts to thicken. Remove from the heat, add the cheeses and allow the residual heat to melt them. Stir in the nutmeg, some salt and pepper and the pancetta. Set aside to cool.

Line a large baking tray with baking paper.

Roll out the puff pastry on a floured surface until it is 5 mm thick. Cut out 16 discs, about 6 cm in diameter. Place eight of the discs on the tray, fill them with the cooled besciamella, then lay the other discs on top to enclose the filling. Press around the edges with a fork to seal.

Lightly beat the egg with the milk in a small bowl, then brush the top of the pastries with the egg wash. Place the cheese bites in the fridge to chill while you preheat your oven to 200°C.

Bake the cheese bites for 20–25 minutes or until puffed and golden and cooked on the bottom. Serve warm or at room temperature.

400 g store-bought frozen butter
    puff pastry, thawed
1 egg
2 tablespoons milk

BESCIAMELLA
50 g pancetta, cubed
1 tablespoon extra-virgin olive oil
3 tablespoons butter
3 tablespoons plain flour,
    plus extra for dusting
250 ml (1 cup) full-cream milk
100 g provolone, cut into
    small cubes
30 g freshly grated parmigiano
pinch of freshly ground nutmeg
salt flakes and freshly ground
    black pepper

MASCARPONE FATTO IN CASA
(HOMEMADE MASCARPONE)

MAKES ABOUT 250 G

Very much like cheese curd (see page 142), mascarpone, Italy's most iconic cream cheese, belongs in the realm of the domestic kitchen. All that's needed is milk, cream, lemon and some muslin cloth – and perhaps a patient disposition, too, as the cooked mixture needs to strain in the fridge overnight until set to a spoonable consistency. It's a very gratifying kitchen project, one that the kids will love and can easily be sold to them as 'fun science'.

Mascarpone suits both sweet and savoury preparations and it can be quite pricey, so having a recipe to create it with simple ingredients and hardly any effort perfectly suits Italian home cooks.

Place a colander over a large bowl and line it with a double layer of muslin cloth.

Pour the milk and cream into a large saucepan and bring to a gentle simmer, just below boiling point (around 90°C). Add the lemon juice and stir continuously for 5–6 minutes, keeping the mixture at a gentle simmer. Cover with a lid and allow to cool for 20 minutes.

Pour the milk mixture into the lined colander and allow to cool to room temperature. Cover with beeswax wrap and place in the fridge overnight.

The next morning the whey will have separated and the soft curds in the muslin will have transformed into mascarpone of a spoonable consistency. Transfer the mascarpone to a glass container fitted with a lid and keep in the fridge for up to 3 days. Pour the whey that has collected in the bowl into a glass jar, cover and store in the fridge for up to 2 days.

NOTE
You can use the mascarpone in tiramisù (see page 276) and the leftover whey makes a great substitute for buttermilk in pancakes, cake batters and scones.

2 litres full-cream milk
500 ml (2 cups) double cream
80 ml (⅓ cup) freshly squeezed
   lemon juice

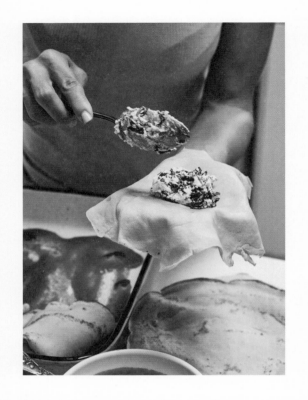

CRESPELLE RICOTTA E SPINACI

(RICOTTA AND SPINACH CRÊPES)

SERVES 4

Crespelle is Italian for crêpes, and these are very popular stuffed and baked until the edges go crispy and the filling is soft and impossibly inviting. However laborious making crêpes sounds, the filling presents no hardship, which I hope is enough to entice you to try this show-stopping favourite.

To make the ricotta and spinach filling, heat the olive oil in a large frying pan over medium heat, add the spinach and garlic, cover and cook until the spinach is just wilted, 2–3 minutes. Set aside to cool and discard the garlic. Combine the ricotta, eggs, cheeses, parsley, lemon zest, nutmeg and some salt and pepper in a bowl. Add the cooled spinach and mix to combine. Cover with beeswax wrap and place in the fridge to firm up for 30 minutes.

Next, to make the tomato sauce, heat the olive oil in a large saucepan over medium heat, add the garlic and fry for 30 seconds or until fragrant. Tip in the tomatoes, then fill each can with water and pour them into the pan. Add the capsicum and celery leaves and bring to a simmer. Add the parsley or basil leaves, turn the heat to low and cook gently for 1 hour. Season with salt and pepper to taste.

Beat the eggs, milk, olive oil and a pinch of salt in a large bowl. Whisk in the flour to create a runny batter. Rest for 20 minutes.

Heat 1 tablespoon of olive oil in a non-stick frying pan over medium heat, then ladle in 2–3 tablespoons of batter to cover the pan in a thin layer. Cook for 1–2 minutes or until the underside is lightly golden, then flip over and cook for another 30 seconds. Set aside on a plate and repeat until all the batter is used (you should have 10–12 crêpes).

Preheat your oven to 200°C.

Ladle a little of the tomato sauce into a 40 cm × 30 cm baking dish. Fill a crêpe with 1–2 tablespoons of the filling, fold into a triangle and place in the dish. Repeat with the rest of the crêpes and filling, making sure you only slightly overlap them in the dish – you want them to be in roughly one layer, so use two baking dishes if needed.

Cover the folded crêpes with 3–4 ladlefuls of tomato sauce (you will have some leftover for a cheeky pasta sauce!). Dust with the parmigiano or pecorino and dot with the butter. Bake for 30–35 minutes or until bubbly and golden and the edges of the crespelle look slightly crispy.

3 eggs
400 ml milk
2 tablespoons olive oil, plus extra for pan-frying
250 g (1⅔ cups) type 00 flour
100 g (1 cup) freshly grated parmigiano or pecorino
a few small cubes of butter

RICOTTA AND SPINACH FILLING
1 tablespoon extra-virgin olive oil
300 g baby spinach leaves
1 garlic clove, skin on, bashed with the back of a knife
300 g fresh ricotta, drained
2 eggs
3 tablespoons freshly grated pecorino
3 tablespoons freshly grated parmigiano
1–2 tablespoons chopped flat-leaf parsley leaves
finely grated zest of ½ lemon
¼ teaspoon freshly ground nutmeg
salt flakes and freshly ground black pepper

TOMATO SAUCE
2 tablespoons extra-virgin olive oil
2 garlic cloves, skin on, bashed with the back of a knife
2 × 400 g cans chopped tomatoes
¼ red capsicum, deseeded
a few celery leaves
a few flat-leaf parsley or basil leaves

FROM

THE

SEA

Italian home cooking and seafood go hand in hand. This is a country geographically blessed with six different seas, each providing abundance and variety. From north to south the local cuisines celebrate what is on offer with respect, creativity and an attitude that perfectly captures the most important principle of Italian home cooking: simplicity.

And while some dishes have show-stopping potential – risotto ai frutti di mare (seafood risotto, see page 176) or tagliolini con gamberi e pomodorini arrosto (handmade noodles with prawns and roasted cherry tomatoes, see page 165) spring to mind – their preparation is void of overly complicated techniques and instead focuses on making the main ingredient the hero at our table, turning a mundane occasion into a very special one.

It was a hard task to keep the number of recipes in this chapter at an acceptable level (the harsh limitations of a book word count!), but you have my word that you will want to make them over and over again, as you will find dishes that are suited for a quick lunch, a shared meal or a more celebratory occasion. These are recipes that have the potential to bring joy to your table, the greatest gift food can provide.

FRITTO MISTO
(CRISPY FRIED PRAWNS, BABY ZUCCHINI AND CALAMARI)

SERVES 4

A sharing plate of deep-fried seafood, brimming with crunchy prawns, calamari and baby zucchini, is hardly ever met with disappointment. This is an Italian seaside classic from time immemorial, best served with lemon wedges and a glass of chilled pinot grigio.

200 g (1⅓ cups) self-raising flour
150 ml ice-cold sparkling water
salt flakes and freshly ground
   black pepper
vegetable oil, for deep-frying
500 g raw school prawns,
   heads removed
4 baby zucchini with their flowers,
   cut in half lengthways and
   stamens removed
8 raw king or banana prawns,
   peeled and deveined, tails intact
2 calamari tubes, cleaned
   and cut into 3 cm squares
lemon wedges, to serve

Mix the flour and sparkling water in a large bowl until a runny batter forms, then season with salt and pepper.

Half fill a large heavy-based frying pan with vegetable oil for deep-frying and heat over medium–high heat to 180°C or until a cube of bread browns in 15 seconds. Line a large plate with paper towel.

Start with the school prawns and zucchini. Dip them in the batter, then shake off the excess. Working in batches, deep-fry the school prawns and zucchini, turning them over to ensure even cooking, for 1–2 minutes or until golden brown and crunchy. Lift them out with a slotted spoon and drain on the paper towel. Repeat the process with the king prawns and calamari, but they'll need a little longer, about 2–3 minutes.

Arrange the fritto misto on a platter and season with salt and pepper. Serve piping hot with lemon wedges.

TAGLIOLINI CON GAMBERI E POMODORINI ARROSTO

(HOMEMADE NOODLES WITH PRAWNS AND ROASTED CHERRY TOMATOES)

SERVES 4

Before you file this away in the too-hard basket, let me assure you there is nothing complicated about this recipe. The pasta can be rolled by hand if a pasta machine is hard to come by, or it can be easily bought from delis and supermarkets, eliminating the need to knead entirely. The sauce is as easy as chopping some tomatoes, mixing them with a few best friends and allowing the oven to do the rest of the work. Then all you need is some juicy prawns and a healthy appetite to scoff this down with gusto.

To make the tagliolini, place the flour on a board, make a well in the centre and drop in the eggs and 1 scant teaspoon of salt. Combine using your fingers or a fork, then knead the mixture vigorously for about 10 minutes. At first it will look crumbly, but once your body heat activates the starch in the flour, the dough will change its texture, turning into a smooth, firm ball. Wrap it in beeswax wrap and refrigerate for 30 minutes. If you want to speed things up, you can mix the dough in a food processor in under 2 minutes. Process the ingredients until they resemble wet sand, then tip onto a floured board, bring together with your hands and knead for 1 minute. (Using store-bought egg tagliolini is absolutely fine, too, by the way.)

After the dough has rested it will feel elastic and very pliable. Dust your board with semolina, then cut the dough into quarters. Work with one piece at a time and keep the rest wrapped to prevent them from drying out. Flatten the dough with the palm of your hand, then pass it through your pasta machine's widest setting three or four times, folding the dough into three each time. Continue passing the dough through the machine (no further folding required), each time through a thinner setting until you get to the second-last setting or the sheet is roughly 2.5 mm thick. Finally, pass the sheet through the spaghetti cutter. Place the noodles on a floured tea towel, dust with the semolina and allow to dry slightly at room temperature.

2 tablespoons extra-virgin olive oil
2 spring onions, finely chopped
1 garlic clove, finely chopped
1 small handful of flat-leaf parsley stalks, finely chopped
12 raw tiger prawns, peeled and deveined, tails intact
150 ml dry white wine
chopped flat-leaf parsley leaves, to serve (optional)
chilli oil, to serve (optional)

TAGLIOLINI
400 g (2⅔ cups) type 00 flour
4 eggs, at room temperature
salt flakes
coarse semolina, for dusting

ROASTED CHERRY TOMATOES
600 g cherry tomatoes
80 ml (⅓ cup) extra-virgin olive oil
3 garlic cloves, skin on, bashed with the back of a knife
1 tablespoon dried oregano
2 spring onions, thinly sliced
1 small handful of flat-leaf parsley stalks (no need to chop them)
pinch of sugar

>

Preheat your oven to 180°C and line a roasting tin with baking paper.

To make the roasted cherry tomatoes, place the tomatoes in a large bowl and add the olive oil, garlic, oregano, spring onion, parsley stalks, sugar and 2 teaspoons of salt. Using your hands, toss the tomatoes in the dressing until nicely coated, then tip them into the tin. Roast for 1–1½ hours or until the tomatoes look slightly sunburnt and are bursting with ripeness. Transfer to a bowl, making sure you collect all the juices – they will make your final dish sing. Discard the wilted parsley stalks, squeeze the soft garlic out of its skin into the tomatoes (discard the skin), then set aside.

Bring a large saucepan of salted water to the boil.

To prepare the prawns, heat the olive oil in a large heavy-based frying pan over medium–high heat. Add the spring onion, garlic and chopped parsley stalks and cook for 2–3 minutes or until fragrant. Add the prawns and 1 teaspoon of salt and cook, stirring with a wooden spoon, for 1 minute. Pour in the wine and allow it to bubble away for 2–3 minutes or until the alcohol has evaporated. Turn off the heat. Add the roasted cherry tomatoes and toss to combine.

Shortly before the cherry tomato and prawn sauce is ready, drop the tagliolini into the boiling water and stir, then cook for 2–3 minutes or until just done. Using tongs, lift the pasta straight into the tomato and prawn pan, along with 3–4 tablespoons of pasta cooking water, and stir the tagliolini in the sauce for 1 minute or until nicely coated in the garlic and wine juices. Serve immediately, with a generous scattering of chopped parsley leaves and a drizzle of chilli oil, if you like.

ZUPPETTA DI COZZE E VONGOLE
(MUSSELS AND CLAMS IN A WHITE WINE BROTH)

SERVES 4

2 tablespoons extra-virgin olive oil

2 garlic cloves, finely chopped

125 g (¾ cup) cherry tomatoes, cut in half

1 small red chilli, thinly sliced

1–2 tablespoons finely chopped flat-leaf parsley stalks

1 kg mussels, scrubbed and debearded (see Note)

1 kg vongole (clams), rinsed in cold water to remove grit

150 ml dry white wine

4 slices of sourdough

salt flakes

flat-leaf parsley leaves, to serve

Imagine yourself seated at a beach kiosk on the Adriatic shore, diving into a bowl of steamy, spicy clams and mussels in a white wine broth, Italian pop music in the background, along with the sound of the waves, children laughing and adults of all ages battling it out at calcietto (foosball). No Italian summer goes by without this postcard image being imprinted in the collective memory.

Heat the olive oil in a large heavy-based saucepan over medium–high heat. Add the garlic, cherry tomatoes, chilli and parsley stalks and stir for about 20–30 seconds or until fragrant. Add the mussels, vongole and wine and allow the alcohol to bubble away for 1–2 minutes, then cover and allow the steam to open the mussels and vongole (this will take 4–5 minutes).

Meanwhile, grill the sourdough to your liking (I love it a little charred).

Once all the mollusc shells have opened, remove the pan from the heat. Discard any broken or unopened shells.

Tip the mussels, vongole and poaching liquid into a large serving bowl and season to taste with salt, if needed. Scatter some parsley leaves on top and serve hot with the grilled sourdough.

NOTE

To debeard the mussels, simply give a firm tug on the furry string dangling from the shells.

COZZE GRATINATE
(STUFFED <u>AND</u> BAKED MUSSELS)

SERVES 4–6 AS A SHARING DISH

Italian home cooks swear by one fundamental rule: never mix cheese and seafood. But we also know that with every rule there's an exception, and, while you'll never encounter an Italian dusting a bowl of spaghetti vongole with parmigiano, along every Italian coastline you will taste delicacies such as this addictive treat of stuffed and baked mussels and wonder where that elusive flavour comes from. Well, it's dairy! In the form of freshly grated peppery pecorino cheese. Be parsimonious though, as the pecorino should be a discreet, aloof presence, allowing the mussels to shine as the one and only hero. Serve hot with a glass of prosecco and get the party started.

Preheat your oven grill. Line a large baking tray with baking paper.

Mix the breadcrumbs, parsley, pecorino, garlic, chilli, olive oil and salt and pepper to taste in a bowl until you have a wet mixture. Set aside.

To prepare your mussels, first throw away any that are broken or open and do not close immediately when they are tapped. Using a sharp paring knife, open the mussels to reveal the mollusc inside. Discard the empty half shell.

Cover each mussel in its half shell with a scant tablespoon of the breadcrumb mixture and press down lightly. Place the filled mussel shells on the tray and grill for 4–5 minutes or until nicely golden on top (watch them carefully as you don't want them to burn).

Arrange on a platter and serve immediately.

60 g (¾ cup) fresh breadcrumbs

⅓ cup finely chopped flat-leaf parsley leaves

3 tablespoons freshly grated pecorino

2 garlic cloves, finely chopped

1 small red chilli, finely chopped

80–100 ml extra-virgin olive oil

salt flakes and freshly ground white pepper

1 kg mussels, scrubbed and debearded (see Note, page 168)

RISONI RISOTTATI CON VONGOLE E POMODORINI

(QUICK RISONI 'RISOTTO' <u>WITH</u> CLAMS <u>AND</u> CHERRY TOMATOES)

SERVES 4

While it's true that cooking pasta in the same style as risotto is quite new to the tradition of Italian home cooking, it is safe to say the method has permanently infiltrated our domestic habits, and it's not surprising to see why. Cooking pasta in the sauce it's going to be dressed with means that every piece of pasta absorbs the flavour of the sauce, elevating a simple tomato pasta to the stratosphere. For those who are less familiar with this concept, it requires no more skill than that needed to make risotto. The pasta is added raw to an initial soffritto (stir-fry) of either onion or spring onion and garlic. Then, just as you would with rice, the liquid goes in and is slowly absorbed by the pasta as it cooks. Risoni is a particularly well-suited pasta shape, the literal translation meaning 'big rice grains'. However, unlike rice, it takes only 7–8 minutes to cook, making this dish a phenomenally speedy dinner option. If you can't find risoni, ditalini also work well.

Place a large heavy-based saucepan or deep frying pan over high heat, add the vongole and wine, cover and cook for 2–3 minutes or until the shells have opened. Drain, reserving the poaching liquid. Set the vongole aside.

Heat the olive oil in the same pan over medium–high heat, add the spring onion, parsley stalks and garlic and cook for 1 minute, watching the garlic closely as it can burn easily. Once it smells fragrant, add the risoni and stir. Deglaze with the reserved poaching liquid, scraping up any bits caught on the base, and allow it to bubble away for 2–3 minutes to cook out the alcohol. Add the cherry tomatoes and vongole and enough water to submerge the baby pasta. Reduce the heat to medium–low, add a pinch of salt and cook for 6–7 minutes or until the risoni is al dente. If you think it looks too liquid, turn the heat up for 1 minute before the end of the cooking time.

Taste for seasoning and adjust to your liking. Serve in shallow bowls with the parsley leaves, a drizzle of extra olive oil, a sprinkle of chilli flakes, if liked, and a grinding of white pepper.

NOTE
If vongole are unavailable, pipis will work just fine.

500 g vongole (clams), rinsed in cold water to remove grit

120 ml dry white wine

3 tablespoons extra-virgin olive oil, plus extra to serve

2 spring onions, finely chopped

1 tablespoon finely chopped flat-leaf parsley stalks

1 garlic clove, finely chopped

350 g risoni

400 g can cherry tomatoes or 500 g fresh cherry tomatoes, cut in half

salt flakes

roughly chopped flat-leaf parsley leaves, to serve

chilli flakes, to serve (optional)

freshly ground white pepper

POLPO CON PISELLI
(BABY OCTOPUS AND PEA STEW)

SERVES 4

3 tablespoons extra-virgin olive oil

1 golden shallot, thinly sliced

600 g cleaned baby octopus (or use cuttlefish tentacles and tubes, cut into bite-sized pieces)

1 garlic clove, crushed

150 ml dry white wine

200 g canned chopped tomatoes

salt flakes and freshly ground black pepper

300 g (2 cups) fresh or frozen peas

2–3 tablespoons finely chopped flat-leaf parsley leaves (optional)

crusty bread, to serve

I am always partial to a dish that comes with its own sauce and side. It is indeed the case with this traditional stew from the Adriatic coast, where cephalopods, traditionally cuttlefish, are gently cooked in a tomato and white wine broth until fork tender. Three-quarters of the way through, peas join the party, adding freshness and sweetness to this delectable dish.

If cuttlefish is hard to come by, squid or baby octopus (pictured here) are excellent alternatives. Serve with plenty of bread – this self-saucing offering begs to be mopped up with gusto! Any unlikely leftovers make a phenomenal pasta dressing.

Heat the olive oil in a large heavy-based frying pan over medium heat. Add the shallot and cook for 1 minute or until fragrant. Add the baby octopus or cuttlefish and cook, stirring once or twice, for 2–3 minutes or until it turns opaque. Stir in the garlic and cook for 30–45 seconds, then pour in the wine and allow it to bubble away for 2–3 minutes to cook out the alcohol. Add the tomatoes, 250 ml (1 cup) of water and a pinch of salt and pepper, then reduce the heat to low. Cover with a lid and simmer for 30 minutes.

Add the peas to the pan and check that the sauce hasn't dried out too much (if so, add 2 teaspoons of water). Cover again and cook for a further 20 minutes or until the octopus or cuttlefish is fork tender.

Serve with a scattering of parsley on top, if you like, and plenty of bread to soak up that spectacular sauce.

RISOTTO AI FRUTTI DI MARE

(SEAFOOD RISOTTO)

SERVES 4

This is a true show stopper, yet intrinsically simple, especially if you are familiar with the basic steps of risotto making. The real magic happens towards the end, when the seafood is added, turning a bowl of rice into a memorable dish. As always with risotto, timing is of the essence. Make sure your guests are ready to receive their bowl of perfectly creamy deliciousness, as risotto needs to be eaten, and honoured, as soon as it's served.

Heat the olive oil and 1 tablespoon of the butter in a large heavy-based frying pan over medium heat. Add the onion and a pinch of salt and cook for a few minutes or until the onion is softened. Add the rice and cook, stirring well, for 1 minute or until the grains are translucent. Pour in the wine and allow it to bubble away for 2–3 minutes or until the alcohol has evaporated.

Turn the heat to medium–low and start adding the stock a ladleful at a time, stirring gently and waiting until the rice has absorbed the stock before adding more. Continue adding the stock and occasionally giving it a gentle stir until the rice is three-quarters cooked, about 13–14 minutes. Add the mussels and keep cooking as before, adding the stock and gently stirring until the mussels have opened and the rice is al dente, another 3–4 minutes.

Turn off the heat. Add the remaining butter and one ladleful of stock. Season to your liking and stir vigorously to release the starch and create the classic all'onda (like a wave) texture. If the mussel shells are in the way, remove them from the pan before stirring, then add them back in. Add the prawns and scallops and stir well to cover the seafood with the rice. Cover and let the risotto rest for 3 minutes to allow the residual heat to just cook the prawns and scallops and to create the perfect mantecatura (creaminess).

Shake the pan, then spoon the risotto into shallow bowls (when risotto is served in deep bowls it keeps cooking and you don't want this). Scatter on the parsley and lemon zest, sprinkle with a little more pepper, if desired, and serve immediately.

2 tablespoons extra-virgin olive oil

3 tablespoons butter

1 small onion, finely chopped

salt flakes and freshly ground black pepper

350 g carnaroli or arborio rice

125 ml (½ cup) dry white wine

2 litres vegetable or fish stock, heated to a gentle simmer

16 mussels, scrubbed and debearded (see Note, page 168)

8 raw king prawns, peeled and deveined

8 scallops, roe removed

2–3 tablespoons finely chopped flat-leaf parsley leaves

finely grated zest of 1 lemon

AN ODE TO ANCHOVIES

Italian home cooks are known for their passion for anchovies. Some may not even show the same devotion to seafood, but when it comes to the salty, oily delicacy that is anchovies, love knows no bounds. Our fervour is such that there should be a setting in dating apps where you can match with other anchovy lovers, just to weed out any haters!

The following recipes are some my favourite ways to enjoy anchovies. As much as we Italians are known to enjoy them simply filleted and swimming in piquant olive oil (with lots of bread on hand), our culinary repertoire extends much further than this to bakes (see page 186), dips (see page 193) and pasta sauces (see page 183). It is no secret that anchovies are also incredible on top of pizza (see page 188) and can add an amazing flavour to salad dressings (see page 194).

If you have not yet been seduced by the unique, multifaceted flavour of anchovies, try disguising a few chopped ones in a lamb roast (see page 210) or in the base for a simple aglio e olio pasta. What you will taste is salt, with an elusive injection of umami. Start small, choose the best quality you can find … and avoid anchovy paste at all costs!

CROSTINI CON ACCIUGHE, POMODORINO E BURRATA

(ANCHOVY, CHERRY TOMATO AND BURRATA CROSTINI)

SERVES 4

If you wish to win the heart of an Italian, present them with a simple crostini topped with sweet tomatoes, salty anchovies and creamy burrata. The flavour and texture combination creates an addiction that can only be satisfied by having more, and then some more ... my kind of aphrodisiac!

Preheat your oven grill.

Brush the baguette slices with 2 tablespoons of the olive oil and toast to your liking under the hot grill.

Meanwhile, place the tomato in a bowl, add the remaining oil, season with salt and pepper to taste and mix well.

Place the grilled bread slices on a serving plate and distribute the tomato mixture among them. Top each slice with a small piece of torn burrata, two anchovies and a few basil leaves, then serve.

8 thin slices of day-old baguette
80 ml (⅓ cup) extra-virgin olive oil
150 g (1 cup) cherry tomatoes, chopped
salt flakes and freshly ground black pepper
1 burrata ball, well drained and torn
16 anchovy fillets in olive oil, drained
baby basil leaves, to serve

BIGOLI IN SALSA
(VENETIAN SPAGHETTI WITH ANCHOVY SAUCE)

SERVES 4

WARNING: this Venetian classic of durum wheat pasta dressed with a salty anchovy sauce requires an all-consuming, burning passion for anchovies! I will concede this punchy dish isn't for the faint-hearted and it may be an acquired taste. Treat it as the Italian version of Vegemite.

Bigoli are a delicious, chubby, spaghetti-style pasta, made with durum wheat flour and water. Rolling them by hand may sound laborious, but it really doesn't take that long and it's a great entry-level homemade pasta shape, especially because bigoli's appeal lies in its rustic look, which means you can relax and not strive for perfection.

To make the bigoli, place the flours and 1 teaspoon of salt in a large bowl, make a well in the centre and slowly pour in the lukewarm water, mixing as you go to incorporate the flour. Don't add all the water at once as you may not need it all; by the same token, you may need to add a little extra water if the dough is too stiff or dry. Using durum wheat flour will probably require a little more liquid than plain flour or specialty pasta flour.

Tip the dough onto a floured surface, oil your hands and knead for about 3–4 minutes or until it comes together in a smooth ball. Add a little extra flour if it feels a bit sticky. Wrap it in beeswax wrap and let it rest at room temperature for 30 minutes. You can make the dough a day ahead, if it's more convenient.

Dust a large board with flour, oil your hands and pinch off a 3 cm × 2 cm piece of dough. Roll it between your hands into a 3–4 mm thick rope. Repeat with the remaining dough. Dust the bigoli with a little flour and set aside.

Bring a large saucepan of salted water to the boil.

Heat the olive oil in a large frying pan over medium–low heat. Add the shallot and a pinch of salt and cook for 3–4 minutes or until the shallot is softened. Add eight of the anchovies and break them up into the sauce with a wooden spoon. Turn off the heat.

Roughly chop the remaining anchovies and set aside.

75 ml extra-virgin olive oil
4 golden shallots, thinly sliced
12 anchovy fillets in olive oil, drained

BIGOLI
250 g durum wheat flour (semolina flour), plain flour or specialty pasta flour, plus extra for dusting
50 g wholemeal flour
salt flakes
225–250 ml lukewarm water
olive oil, to grease your hands

>

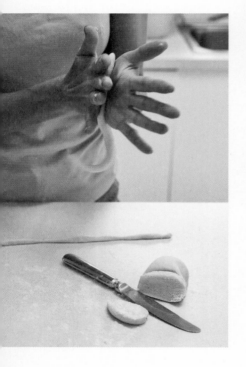

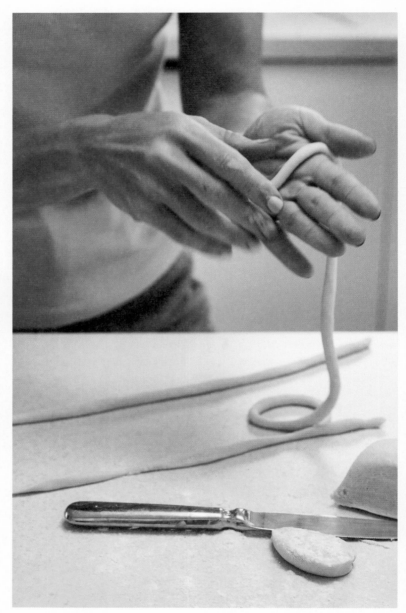

Once the water is boiling, drop in the bigoli and stir well. Cook the bigoli until it is al dente, about 5–6 minutes. Using a spaghetti spoon or tongs, transfer the bigoli to the anchovy sauce. Turn the heat to medium–low, toss well to combine and add 2–3 tablespoons of pasta cooking water or as much as you need to thin out the sauce and create a creamy texture. Divide the pasta among bowls and top with the reserved chopped anchovies.

NOTE
If you are pressed for time, store-bought dried casarecce will work just fine instead of bigoli. It will take about 8–9 minutes to cook until al dente.

TIAN DI ACCIUGHE
(OVEN-BAKED ANCHOVIES)

SERVES 4

Think filleted anchovies snugly nestled within layers of cherry tomatoes, olives and breadcrumbs . . . 15 minutes in a hot oven is enough to cook them through and create an inviting crunchy top. This is an inexpensive yet truly extraordinary meal that the frugal Italian home cook will always welcome at the table. Serve hot or warm with crusty bread, vino and a smile. If whole anchovies are not available, look for small sardines.

Preheat your oven to 200°C. Oil a small baking dish and sprinkle with some breadcrumbs.

Place half the anchovies in the dish to line the base, then top with half the cherry tomatoes, half the garlic, half the olives and half the breadcrumbs. Sprinkle on some dried oregano and season with salt and pepper, then drizzle on half the olive oil. Repeat this process with the remaining anchovies, tomatoes, garlic, olives and breadcrumbs, season and drizzle on the remaining olive oil to make a second layer.

Bake the anchovies for 15–20 minutes or until cooked through and beautifully golden on top.

NOTE
To make your own fresh breadcrumbs, save your stale bread and simply blitz it in a food processor until crumbs form.

50 g fresh breadcrumbs (see Note), plus extra to sprinkle

16 fresh anchovies (small sardines can also be used), filleted and split down the middle (ask your fishmonger to do this)

300 g (2 cups) cherry tomatoes, cut in half

1–2 garlic cloves, thinly sliced

2–3 tablespoons pitted black olives

dried oregano, to taste

salt flakes and freshly ground black pepper

75 ml extra-virgin olive oil

SFINCIONE SICILIANO

(SICILIAN ANCHOVY AND TOMATO DEEP-PAN PIZZA)

SERVES 6

Anchovy on pizza is no ground-breaking culinary discovery, but it certainly is the one topping that always gets my vote. Sfincione is not your regular, thin-crusted pizza – this Sicilian street food takes its name from the local dialect 'sfincia' (soffice), which means soft. The dough has a bouncy, spongy texture, and is topped with tomato, oregano and salty anchovies.

To make the pizza dough, mix the yeast and 400 ml of the lukewarm water in a bowl and stand for a few minutes to froth up. Tip the flours into a large bowl, add the yeast mixture and mix for 1–2 minutes or until the dough comes together. Add 3 teaspoons of salt and knead lightly to incorporate. If the dough feels too dry, add the remaining 25 ml of water. Knead the dough on a lightly floured surface for 5–7 minutes or until smooth (you can also use an electric mixer fitted with the dough hook for this). Shape the dough into a ball, place it in an oiled bowl and drizzle a little olive oil on top to prevent a crust forming. Cover with a damp tea towel and rest at room temperature for 30 minutes or until the dough is very relaxed and smooth.

Using floured hands, stretch the dough into a 50 cm × 40 cm rectangle. Fold the top and bottom thirds into the centre, like you are folding a letter, then fold the dough onto itself into a ball. Cover with a damp tea towel and rest at room temperature for 3–4 hours or until doubled in size.

Meanwhile, heat the olive oil in a large frying pan over medium heat, add the onion and a pinch of salt and pepper and cook for 2–3 minutes or until softened. Add the tomatoes and some extra salt and cook for 20 minutes until slightly reduced. Set aside.

Preheat your oven to 200°C. Oil a large baking dish.

Punch down the dough and knead briefly on a lightly floured surface to expel any air bubbles. Stretch out with your hands until 1.5 cm thick, then place in the dish. Top with the tomato mixture, oregano, cheese, breadcrumbs and a drizzle of olive oil. Bake for 25–30 minutes or until golden. Top with the anchovies and enjoy hot, warm or at room temperature.

NOTE

Caciocavallo is a type of Italian cheese that melts beautifully. It is used in many types of dishes, especially pasta bakes and toasted sandwiches or pizza.

2 tablespoons extra-virgin olive oil, plus extra for drizzling
1 onion, thinly sliced
400 g can chopped tomatoes
freshly ground black pepper
1–2 tablespoons dried oregano
80 g freshly grated hard cheese, such as caciocavallo (see Note), pecorino or aged dried provolone
50 g dried breadcrumbs
6–8 anchovy fillets in olive oil, drained

PIZZA DOUGH

2 teaspoons dried yeast
400–425 ml lukewarm water
450 g (3 cups) type 00 flour, plus extra for dusting
100 g durum wheat flour (semolina flour)
salt flakes

BAGNA CAUDA PIEMONTESE

(PIEDMONT-STYLE ANCHOVY AND GARLIC DIP)

SERVES 4–6

The name 'bagna cauda' is local Piemontese vernacular for 'bagno caldo' (hot bath), a reminder that this dip is best served hot.

The combination of anchovies melted into a potent garlicky oil speaks to the hearts of those who fervently adore pungent flavours. My only advice when it comes to consuming this addictive dip would be to perhaps limit your romantic endeavours for a few days after (as the aromas tend to linger) . . . unless, of course, your lover has indulged in this delicacy as well.

Remove and discard the green centre (germ) from the garlic cloves, then slice the garlic very thinly (or grate on a microplane). Combine the garlic and milk in a small saucepan and cook over low heat for 5 minutes. Remove the pan from the heat and allow the garlic to infuse the warm milk for 1 hour.

Place the olive oil and butter in a small saucepan over low heat. Add the garlic and milk mixture and the anchovies and cook gently, stirring with a wooden spoon, for 10–15 minutes or until the anchovies have melted into the sauce. Don't let the mixture come to the boil.

Strain through a fine sieve and pour the bagna cauda into a serving bowl. Serve either hot or at room temperature with the raw or blanched vegetables for dipping.

NOTES

One thing I have learned when handling copious amounts of garlic is to cut the cloves in half and remove the small green heart, which in Italy is referred to as 'l'anima' (the soul). Removing it makes the final dish easier to digest (and perhaps easier on your breath, too!).

Bagna cauda will naturally tend to separate into oil and milk solids. Just mix before using.

4–5 garlic cloves, bashed with the
  back of a knife and peeled
200 ml full-cream milk
100 ml extra-virgin olive oil
30 g butter
8 anchovy fillets in olive oil, drained
raw or blanched vegetables, to serve
  (try radishes, Dutch carrots, baby
  zucchini, celery hearts, thinly
  sliced fennel, baby artichokes,
  cherry tomatoes, treviso and
  witlof leaves)

INSALATA DI CAVOLFIORE CRUDO

(RAW CAULIFLOWER SALAD WITH ANCHOVY DRESSING)

SERVES 4–6

100 ml extra-virgin olive oil

finely grated zest and juice of
  1 lemon

6 anchovy fillets in olive oil, drained
  and chopped

35 g (¼ cup) capers, rinsed, drained
  and roughly chopped

40 g (¼ cup) pitted kalamata olives,
  finely chopped

1 golden shallot, thinly sliced

½ bunch of flat-leaf parsley, leaves
  picked and roughly chopped

1 large head of cauliflower, thinly
  sliced with a mandoline

freshly ground black pepper

If you are new to the joy of a raw cauliflower salad, I urge you to give this one a try. The trick is to cut the head into thin slices; alternatively, you can chop it into very small, blueberry-sized pieces.

The dressing makes this dish the superstar it is, with the salty, zesty kick provided by the anchovies and capers. It's an understated show stopper.

Place the olive oil, lemon zest and juice, anchovies, capers, olives, shallot and parsley in a jar. Seal, then shake to combine.

Arrange the cauliflower on a platter, drizzle with the dressing and season with pepper to serve.

PESCE AL SALE CON SALMORIGLIO AI CAPPERI

(SALT-BAKED FISH WITH HERB AND CAPER DRESSING)

SERVES 4

This recipe features the classic Italian method of baking a whole fish under a crust of salty dough. It's so brilliant it is mostly served by itself drizzled with olive oil, or with a zesty salmoriglio (a fresh dressing of lemon, herbs and garlic). This cooking method is a lot simpler than it seems – the fish, subtly flavoured with herbs, steams under its shield and the result is delicate, pearly flesh. Because of its audacious simplicity, it is crucial to source the freshest fish you can get your hands on. The flesh of male snapper tends to be more succulent than that of females. You can easily tell a male by the big bump on top of his head. Barramundi is a good alternative to snapper – use whichever looks best on the day.

500 g (2 cups) fine salt

300 g (2 cups) plain flour, plus extra if needed

4 egg whites

1 lemon, cut into quarters, plus 4 thin slices of lemon

2 × 400 g whole snapper, scaled and gutted (or 1 large one)

2 garlic cloves, bashed with the back of a knife and peeled

2 large handfuls of flat-leaf parsley leaves

SALMORIGLIO AI CAPPERI

2 tablespoons freshly squeezed lemon juice

3 tablespoons extra-virgin olive oil

1 teaspoon salt flakes

2 tablespoons capers, drained and roughly chopped

1½ teaspoons chopped flat-leaf parsley leaves

½ teaspoon fresh or dried oregano

½ garlic clove, crushed

Preheat your oven to 220°C. Line a large baking dish with baking paper.

Put the salt in a food processor and blitz for 3–4 seconds. Add the flour and egg whites and pulse until wet crumbs form. Feel the dough with your fingers and add 3–4 tablespoons of water if it's too dry. Blitz again until the dough comes away from the side of the bowl. You're after a pliable dough that's soft but not sticky. Add a little extra flour if your dough is wet. Roll out the dough on a floured surface to a thickness of about 1 cm and cut it into two sheets.

Place the lemon quarters and fish in the dish. Fill the cavities of the fish with the lemon slices, garlic and parsley leaves. Lay a salt dough sheet over each fish and lightly tuck it in. Bake for 20–25 minutes.

Meanwhile, make the salmoriglio. Whisk the lemon juice, olive oil and salt in a small bowl. Mix in the capers, herbs and garlic and leave to infuse.

Check the fish by gently lifting the dough crust. If the skin peels off to reveal pearly flesh that easily comes away from the bone, the fish is done. If not, return to the oven for another 2–3 minutes.

To serve, lift off the salt crust and discard. Use a spoon and fork to carefully lift the flesh on one side off the fish and transfer to a serving plate. Now the backbone is revealed and you can easily lift it up in one piece and discard it. The remaining side of the fish is ready to transfer to a plate. Serve one side of snapper per plate along with a generous drizzle of salmoriglio.

PESCE ALL'ACQUA PAZZA

(MEDITERRANEAN POACHED FISH)

SERVES 4

The literal translation of this dish is 'fish in mad water', the madness being a delectable tomato, wine and olive oil broth that gently poaches white fish fillets. More than madness, this method of cooking fish seems to thoroughly embrace the spirit of Italian home cooking, where a few ingredients create a sensational meal that will make you love it 'alla follia' (like crazy).

Heat the olive oil in a large heavy-based frying pan over medium heat. Add the spring onion, garlic and chilli flakes and cook for 1–2 minutes or until softened. Add the cherry tomatoes, stir well and cook for 1 minute, then pour in the wine and allow it to bubble away for 2–3 minutes to cook out the alcohol.

Add 150 ml of water to the tomato mixture, season with salt and pepper and add the fish. Turn the heat to low, cover and cook gently for 3–4 minutes or until the fish is almost cooked through. Remove the pan from the heat and let the fish rest in its poaching liquid with the lid on for another 5 minutes to allow the residual heat to finish cooking it.

Divide the fish and poaching liquid among serving bowls, scatter on the parsley and some extra spring onion, if desired, and serve with lots of bread for mopping up the delicious juices.

3 tablespoons extra-virgin olive oil

2 spring onions, pale green and white parts thinly sliced, plus extra to serve

2 garlic cloves, bashed with the back of a knife, skin on or off

tip of a teaspoon of chilli flakes

150 g (1 cup) cherry tomatoes, cut in half

150 ml dry white wine

salt flakes and freshly ground black pepper

4 × 200 g monkfish fillets (or any other white fish), skin removed and pin-boned, cut into large chunks

finely chopped flat-leaf parsley leaves, to serve

crusty bread, to serve

DENTICE AL FORNO CON PATATE, POMODORINI, OLIVE E CAPPERI

(WHOLE SNAPPER <u>WITH</u> POTATOES, CHERRY TOMATOES, OLIVES <u>AND</u> CAPERS)

SERVES 4

125 g (¾ cup) cherry tomatoes, cut in half

90 g (½ cup) pitted black olives

1–2 tablespoons capers, rinsed and drained

3–4 anchovy fillets in olive oil, drained

125 ml (½ cup) dry white wine

100 ml extra-virgin olive oil

3 potatoes, boiled and cut into wedges

salt flakes

1 × 1 kg whole snapper, scaled and gutted, scored with two slashes on each side

roughly chopped flat-leaf parsley leaves, to serve

The idea with this dish is to create a tasty bed for a whole fish to nestle on. As it all bakes, the juices, flavours and aromas combine to create the most delicious one-pan dinner. Watch out for those coveted potatoes . . . they are sensational, having absorbed all the pan juices like golden sponges.

Preheat your oven to 180°C. Oil a large baking dish.

Place the cherry tomatoes, olives, capers, anchovies, wine and half the olive oil in the dish. Add the potato, season with salt and toss with the other ingredients. Bake for 10 minutes, then remove from the oven.

Place the snapper on the cherry tomato mixture and baste with the pan juices, drizzling them onto the slashes cut into the flesh. Season with a little more salt and return to the oven. Bake for a further 20–25 minutes or until the fish is just cooked through. To test if it's ready, gently lift some flesh with a butter knife. If it lifts off easily and looks opaque, the fish is done. Scatter some parsley over the top, drizzle on the remaining olive oil and serve.

POLENTA CON FRUTTI DI MARE

(SEAFOOD STEW WITH SOFT POLENTA)

SERVES 4

3 tablespoons extra-virgin olive oil

2 garlic cloves, finely chopped

2 tablespoons finely chopped
    flat-leaf parsley leaves

100 ml dry white wine

400 g can chopped tomatoes

2 litres vegetable stock

300 g ling or barramundi fillets,
    skin removed and pin-boned,
    cut into 3 cm pieces

12 raw banana prawns, peeled
    and deveined, tails intact

8 scallops, roe removed

8 mussels, scrubbed and debearded
    (see Note, page 168)

8 vongole (clams), rinsed in cold
    water to remove grit

salt flakes

250 g (1⅔ cups) instant polenta

chilli oil or finely chopped red chilli,
    to serve (optional)

This is an adaptation of my nonna's famous polenta and sausage stew, which she used to serve on a large wooden board straight to the table. I've swapped the sturdy meat sauce for a delicate seafood one, served in individual bowls on a bed of soft polenta. The polenta absorbs all the juices and leaves anyone who eats it gobsmacked.

Heat the olive oil in a large heavy-based saucepan over medium–high heat. Add the garlic and parsley and cook, stirring, for 1–2 minutes or until fragrant. Add the wine and let it bubble away for 2–3 minutes or until it has evaporated. Add the tomatoes and stock and bring to a simmer, then reduce the heat to medium–low and cook for 20–30 minutes or until reduced and slightly thickened.

Add the fish and prawns to the pan and cook for 1 minute. Add the remaining seafood, cover with a lid and cook, shaking the pan once or twice, for a further 1–2 minutes or until the mussels and vongole have opened and the seafood is just cooked through. Remove from the heat.

Pour 750 ml (3 cups) of water into a saucepan and bring to the boil. Add 2 teaspoons of salt, turn the heat to low and slowly rain in the polenta, stirring constantly with a whisk to prevent lumps forming. Continue to cook gently, stirring, for 1–2 minutes. Remove from the heat.

Divide the soft polenta among shallow bowls, top with the seafood stew and serve straight away with a drizzle of chilli oil or a sprinkle of chilli if you like it hot.

P

N°. 5
POULTRY & MEAT

OULTRY

MEAT

While Italian home cooking owes its fame to the myriad pasta dishes so universally loved, the country's food legacy is far richer than its pasta repertoire and boasts many memorable culinary creations that feature meat.

Most of these dishes rely on the boldness of simply grilling the meat to perfection and serving it with bitter greens on the side, or gently stewing cheaper cuts with only a few other ingredients until they meld together in the pot and a knife is no longer needed. Even though they may be uncomplicated in nature, these recipes reward home cooks and those at the table enjoying their flavours time and time again.

I know for a fact that when I announce to my family that cotoletta (Milanese-style veal schnitzel, see page 213) is on the menu, I am met with giddy excitement, or if I have a pot of slowly stewing osso buco (see page 219) or stracotto (Northern Italian–style pot roast, see page 216) on the stove, the anticipation of those succulent morsels is enough to make friends tremble.

As for me, what truly sparks my heart with life is the joy of sharing these dishes, knowing they will be received with love.

POLLO ALLA CACCIATORA
(HUNTER-STYLE CHICKEN STEW)

SERVES 4

80 ml (⅓ cup) extra-virgin olive oil

4 chicken marylands

2 golden shallots, thinly sliced

1 celery stalk, thinly sliced

1 carrot, finely chopped

1 garlic clove, finely chopped

150 ml dry white wine

600 g passata

40 g (¼ cup) pitted black olives

40 g (¼ cup) capers, in vinegar
    or salt, rinsed and drained

1–2 flat-leaf parsley sprigs

salt flakes and freshly ground
    black pepper

2 tablespoons finely chopped
    flat-leaf parsley leaves

crusty sourdough, boiled new
    potatoes or Soft Polenta (see
    page 216), to serve (optional)

This quintessential chicken dish resides proudly in every Italian recipe collection as its one-pot/self-saucing characteristics are the bread and butter of home cooks. Like most popular Italian recipes, pinning down its regional origins is no easy feat, several cities and hamlets on the peninsula boast a version of this peasant dish. Its name suggests the dish originated among communities of hunters (cacciatori), who favoured these simple steps when cooking this stew outdoors in camps during game season. A more ancient version featuring rabbit is also quite popular among my people. However, in memory of my late house bunny Hazel, I tend to stick to poultry when making this satisfying meal.

Heat 2 tablespoons of the olive oil in a large heavy-based saucepan over medium–high heat. Add the chicken marylands and brown on both sides for 3–4 minutes. Transfer the chicken to a bowl and set aside.

Add the remaining oil to the pan and reduce the heat to medium. Add the shallot, celery and carrot and cook for 1–2 minutes or until softened. Stir in the garlic and cook for 30 seconds or until fragrant. Return the chicken to the pan and deglaze with the wine, scraping up any bits caught on the base. Allow it to bubble away for 1–2 minutes to cook out the alcohol. Add the passata, 200 ml of water, the olives, capers and parsley sprigs. Don't add any seasoning as the olives and capers are quite salty. Reduce the heat to low, cover and cook for 35–40 minutes or until the chicken is just cooked through.

Remove the lid, increase the heat to medium and simmer for 5 minutes or until the sauce is thickened. Taste for seasoning and adjust with salt and pepper. Top with the chopped parsley and serve as is or with some crusty sourdough, boiled potatoes or soft polenta.

AGNELLO AL FORNO CON PATATE

(ROAST SHOULDER OF LAMB WITH GARLIC, ROSEMARY AND POTATOES)

SERVES 6–8

This timeless dish is also known in Rome and Central Italy as abbacchio arrosto, and is generally on offer come springtime, when lamb is abundant. This time of the year in Italy also coincides with Easter, and most Italians reserve this one-tray wonder to mark this religious occasion.

There are no particular tricks here, with only a few ingredients needed to create this tasty roast, but in the best home-cooking tradition, I advise you to source your meat ethically and to rely on beautiful extra-virgin olive oil and a good drop of dry white wine to build up the pan juices that are absorbed by the potatoes, which you and your dinner guests will inevitably fight for.

Preheat your oven to 150°C.

With a sharp knife, randomly cut the shoulder of lamb in five or six places, then stuff each cut with some sliced garlic, a few rosemary leaves and an anchovy. Rub half the olive oil over the lamb, then season the entire shoulder with salt and pepper.

Tip the potato into a bowl, toss with the remaining olive oil and season with salt.

Place the lamb in a large deep roasting tin and scatter the potato around it. Cover with foil and roast for 3 hours. Remove the foil, increase the oven temperature to 180°C and continue roasting for 45–60 minutes or until the potatoes are golden and crunchy and the lamb is beautifully cooked through but still succulent.

Place the lamb and potato on a serving platter and serve with a drizzle of the pan juices.

1 × 1 kg shoulder of lamb

5–6 garlic cloves, thinly sliced

5–6 rosemary sprigs

5–6 anchovies

100 ml extra-virgin olive oil

salt flakes and freshly ground white pepper

1 kg chat potatoes, unpeeled and cut in half

COTOLETTA ALLA MILANESE
(MILANESE-STYLE VEAL SCHNITZEL)

SERVES 4

Who doesn't love schnitzel? The mere thought of that crunchy outer coating encasing juicy meat is enough to make me swoon …

Growing up in Milan, the rightful birthplace of cotoletta alla Milanese, I was never short of this regional dish, and even my proud Abruzzese nonna added this northern Italian dish to her arsenal of recipes to please the family on special occasions.

When it comes to cotoletta, Italian home cooks tend to firmly divide themselves into two camps: Team Orecchia di Elefante and Team Costoletta. The first refers to the shape of the veal cut, pounded so thinly it expands in circumference to resemble an elephant's ear (okay, use your imagination here), the latter uses a thick cut, veal rib-eye on the bone, cooked to crunchy perfection, the meat left a blushing shade of pink. This is the way my friends Giovanni and Marco have presented cotoletta at their renowned Milanese restaurant Osteria del Nuovo Macello since the 1990s. And I can safely say I have not tasted a better one since!

First, prepare your workstation. Place three shallow bowls on your bench, add the flour to one, the beaten egg to another and the breadcrumbs to the third. Line a tray with baking paper.

Pat the veal chops dry with paper towel. Dip each chop in the flour, then in the beaten egg, letting any excess drip off, and finally coat entirely and evenly in the breadcrumbs. Place on the tray.

Heat the clarified butter and oil in a large heavy-based frying pan over medium heat. Add the chops and fry for 5–6 minutes each side until golden brown. Drain on paper towel, season with plenty of salt and pepper and serve immediately with lemon wedges and a crisp green salad.

NOTE
If your frying pan is not large enough to accommodate four chops, you can use two small ones and divide the clarified butter and olive oil between the two.

200 g (1⅓ cups) plain flour
2 eggs, beaten
150 g dried breadcrumbs
4 veal rib-eye chops
150 g clarified butter (ghee)
2½ tablespoons olive oil
salt flakes and freshly ground
    black pepper
lemon wedges and green salad,
    to serve

SALTIMBOCCA ALLA ROMANA
(ROMAN-STYLE VEAL WITH SAGE AND PROSCIUTTO)

SERVES 4

The name of this classic Roman dish pretty much explains how delicious it is. Saltimbocca literally means 'jumps in the mouth', and I can guarantee this is going to be your wish the second you are presented with succulent veal delicately wrapped in savoury, crisp prosciutto and sage, and drizzled with wine-infused pan juices. The fact that this takes only 20 minutes to make should be enough for you to immediately bookmark this page.

Beat the veal steaks with a mallet until thin, then cut each steak into three pieces. Press a slice of prosciutto onto each piece, then place a sage leaf on top. Fold the meat to half enclose the prosciutto and sage, trying to keep it nice and flat.

Place the flour in a shallow bowl. Line a baking tray with baking paper. Dip each steak in the flour, shake off the excess, then place on a platter.

Heat the olive oil and butter in a large heavy-based frying pan over medium heat. Add the garlic and as many extra sage leaves as you like, then add the veal, sage leaf–side down, and cook for 3–4 minutes or until the prosciutto is crisp. Turn and cook for 1–2 minutes or until the veal is almost cooked through. Add the wine to the pan and deglaze, scraping up any bits caught on the base. Cook out the alcohol for 1–2 minutes.

Transfer the saltimbocca to a platter, drizzle over the pan juices and serve straight away with your choice of sourdough, lemon wedges and fresh green leaves.

4 × 200 g veal minute steaks

4 thin slices of prosciutto di Parma, cut in half

12 sage leaves, plus extra as desired

150 g (1 cup) plain flour

2½ tablespoons extra-virgin olive oil

25 g butter

1 garlic clove, bashed with the back of a knife

150 ml dry white wine

sourdough, lemon wedges and green leaves, to serve (optional)

STRACOTTO DI MANZO
(NORTHERN ITALIAN–STYLE POT ROAST)

SERVES 4

Italian home cooking is plentiful and varied, the miraculous compound of 21 regions each eager to protect and showcase its character and heritage. The further north you travel, closer to the border with France on one side and Switzerland and Austria on the other, the more likely you are to be exposed to phenomenal food featuring slow-cooked meats, such as this pot roast with the unassuming name of stracotto (super cooked). It may sound like the Italian word for hangover, but ultimately it refers to the cooking time. In this case, the meat is simmered gently in a soffritto and red wine broth until it is so soft you don't need a knife to cut through it, and the sauce is so velvety rich that one taste reminds you of how incredible home cooking can be. Serve with soft polenta for ultimate pleasure.

Heat 2 tablespoons of the olive oil in a large flameproof casserole dish over medium heat. Add the pancetta and steak and brown for 2–3 minutes. Transfer to a bowl and set aside.

Add the remaining olive oil to the dish, then add the onion, carrot, celery and garlic and cook, stirring occasionally, for 5 minutes or until softened. Return the pancetta and steak to the dish and deglaze with the wine, scraping up any bits caught on the base. Allow it to bubble away for 1–2 minutes to cook out the alcohol. Add the stock and tomato paste and season to taste with salt and pepper. Bring to a simmer, then reduce the heat to low and cover with a lid. Braise, turning the steak occasionally, for 4 hours or until it is fork tender. Taste for seasoning and adjust accordingly.

Meanwhile, to make the soft polenta, bring 3 litres of salted water to a simmer in a large saucepan. Slowly rain in the polenta, whisking constantly to prevent any lumps forming. Reduce the heat to low and cook, stirring frequently, for 3–4 minutes or until silky and not at all grainy. Season to taste with a little salt and stir in the parmigiano, keeping in mind that the polenta will soon be coated with the stew, so take care not to overdo it.

Spoon a ladleful or two of polenta into each bowl, top with the stracotto and season with pepper.

3 tablespoons extra-virgin olive oil

100 g pancetta, cut into cubes

850 g chuck steak, cut into chunks

2 onions, finely chopped

2 carrots, diced

2 celery stalks, diced

2 garlic cloves, finely chopped

400 ml red wine

750 ml (3 cups) good-quality beef or vegetable stock

2 tablespoons tomato paste

salt flakes and freshly ground black pepper

SOFT POLENTA

400 g (2⅔ cups) instant polenta

2 tablespoons freshly grated parmigiano

OSSO BUCO CON GREMOLATA E CREMA DI CANNELLINI

(OSSO BUCO WITH GREMOLATA AND CANNELLINI MASH)

SERVES 4

This northern Italian culinary jewel is as close as a recipe comes to magic. Take a cheap cut of meat wrapped around thick bone, stew it slowly and gently alongside carrot, celery and onion and watch the transformation occur. Toughness, surrendering to gentle heat, turns into melting softness, and the bone encloses that most coveted morsel of all, the marrow, which is at once sweet and savoury. Osso buco is traditionally served with risotto or soft polenta, but I would love you to try this nutritious alternative: my quick and delicate cannellini mash that balances out the robustness of the meat.

Season the osso buco with salt and pepper. Heat 3 tablespoons of the olive oil in a large flameproof casserole dish over high heat. Add the osso buco, in batches if need be, and brown on each side for 2–3 minutes. Set aside.

Heat the remaining oil in the dish over medium heat, add the onion, carrot, garlic and bay leaves and cook until the onion is softened. Increase the heat to medium–high and deglaze with the wine, scraping up any bits caught on the base, for 1–2 minutes. Stir in the stock and tomato paste and bring to the boil. Reduce the heat to low and return the osso buco to the dish. Taste for seasoning and adjust accordingly. Cover and simmer for 2½–3 hours or until the meat easily comes away from the bone. Remove the osso buco, paying attention not to separate it from the marrow. Increase the heat to high and reduce the sauce for 5–8 minutes. Return the osso buco to the dish. Set aside.

To make the cannellini mash, heat the olive oil in a saucepan over medium heat, add the onion and garlic and cook for 1 minute or until fragrant. Add the cannellini beans and cook for 3–4 minutes, adding 1–2 tablespoons of water, if needed. Season to taste. Blitz the mixture in a food processor until smooth, adding a little water if it is too stiff.

Place all the gremolata ingredients in a small bowl and mix well.

Spoon the cannellini mash onto serving plates and arrange the osso buco on top, then drizzle on the cooking juices and scatter on the gremolata.

4 × 400 g veal osso buco, dredged
  in plain flour
salt flakes and freshly ground
  black pepper
100 ml extra-virgin olive oil
2 onions, finely chopped
1 carrot, finely chopped
1 garlic clove, finely chopped
1–2 bay leaves
250 ml (1 cup) dry white wine
500 ml (2 cups) good-quality
  chicken or vegetable stock
1 tablespoon tomato paste

CANNELLINI MASH

2 tablespoons extra-virgin olive oil
1 onion, thinly sliced
1 garlic clove, finely chopped
2 × 400 g cans cannellini beans,
  rinsed and drained

GREMOLATA

1 garlic clove, finely chopped
3–4 tablespoons finely chopped
  flat-leaf parsley leaves
finely grated zest of 1 lemon

TAGLIATA DI MANZO CON POMODORINI ARROSTO

(BEEF WITH ROASTED CHERRY TOMATOES)

SERVES 4

Tagliata is Italian for 'sliced', which is exactly how this T-bone is served. The choice of cut is not accidental, as T-bone offers a robust rib-eye on one side and tender fillet on the other, to accommodate each preference. The accompaniment of roasted cherry tomatoes is as delicious as it is stunning, a triumph of colour, texture and flavour, all delivering a show-stopping dish that is very easy to create at home.

Of course, you can use any other type of steak for this dish, from sirloin to flank. And if you are short of time or tomatoes, a simple drizzle of balsamic vinegar and extra-virgin olive oil on those succulent, slightly caramelised slices is the go in most Italian households.

Preheat your oven to 180°C.

Place the cherry tomatoes and garlic in a baking dish, drizzle over the olive oil and balsamic vinegar, season with salt and pepper, scatter on the basil leaves and toss well to combine. Bake for 30–40 minutes or until the tomato is soft and juicy and the garlic cloves are soft. Take the dish out of the oven and set aside to cool a little. Remove the skins from the garlic cloves, smash them with a fork into the tomato juices and mix roughly. Discard the wilted basil leaves. Set aside.

Season the steak generously with the extra-virgin olive oil and salt and pepper on both sides.

Place a chargrill pan over high heat and allow it to get super hot. Add the steak and sear, without turning, for 4 minutes. Turn and cook for a further 3 minutes for rare or 4 minutes for medium–rare. Alternatively, cook as needed if you like yours well done. Transfer the steak to a wire rack over a plate, loosely cover with foil and rest for 6–8 minutes.

Cut the steak into 5 mm thick slices and arrange on a heated platter or board with the roasted cherry tomatoes and their juices liberally drizzled on top. Season with salt and pepper as needed.

800 g cherry tomatoes, cut in half
(you can keep some on the vine
for presentation, if you like)
2–3 garlic cloves, skin on, bashed
with the back of a knife
2 tablespoons olive oil
2 tablespoons balsamic vinegar
salt flakes and freshly ground
black pepper
handful of basil leaves
1 kg T-bone steak
2 tablespoons extra-virgin olive oil

POLPETTONE IN UMIDO
(BRAISED MEATLOAF)

SERVES 4

Humble meatballs hardly need an introduction. Rissoles – or polpette, as we call them in Italy – incapsulate all that is good and comforting about honest home cooking, combining inexpensive everyday ingredients to create a luscious morsel sure to please the whole family. Their versatility in the kitchen is rather impressive, too, and they can range in size from mini ones, perfect as finger food, to larger ones that can be served with mashed potatoes or soft polenta, or this single giant meatball, the much-adored polpettone, shaped into a loaf and braised in a perfumed white wine sauce.

First, place the bread, parmigiano and parsley leaves in a food processor and blitz until combined and coarsely chopped. Tip the mixture into a large bowl and add the ricotta, mince, half the lemon zest, the nutmeg and egg and season with salt and pepper. Amalgamate using your hands until all the ingredients are nicely mixed.

Place a large sheet of baking paper on your work surface. Turn the meat mixture out onto the paper and, with wet hands, shape it into a log about 40 cm × 10 cm. Wrap the paper around the log, then twist to enclose the ends, as if wrapping a giant lolly. Place in the fridge for 20–30 minutes.

Heat the olive oil in a large heavy-based frying pan over medium–high heat, add the onion, carrot and celery and fry for 2–3 minutes. Unwrap the meatloaf, dust with the flour and brown gently on all sides for 2–3 minutes. Deglaze the pan with the wine, scraping up any bits caught on the base. Allow it to bubble away for 1–2 minutes to cook out the alcohol. Pour in the stock, reduce the heat to low and cover with a lid. Simmer for 25–30 minutes or until the polpettone is cooked through. Set aside to cool in the pan for 20 minutes.

Gently lift the polpettone onto a serving plate. Pour the sauce into a blender and whiz for 10–15 seconds or until smooth, then transfer to a serving bowl. Cut the polpettone into thick slices, sprinkle with the remaining lemon zest and some chopped parsley and serve with the sauce.

3 slices of stale sourdough

80 g parmigiano, cut into chunks

handful of flat-leaf parsley leaves

150 g fresh ricotta, well drained

400 g pork and veal mince

finely grated zest of 2 lemons

½ teaspoon freshly ground nutmeg

1 egg

salt flakes and freshly ground black pepper

3 tablespoons extra-virgin olive oil

1 small onion, finely chopped

1 small carrot, diced

1 small celery stalk, thinly sliced

plain flour, for dusting

150 ml dry white wine

250 ml (1 cup) good-quality chicken or vegetable stock

chopped flat-leaf parsley, to serve

BREAD

SWEET

Nº. 6
BREAD, SWEETS & COFFEE

Italian confectionery is simple and unadorned, an unpretentious combination of prime ingredients and masterful techniques that need hardly any embellishment. It seems like Italian bakers feel no pressure to seduce the customers with complex constructions of multilayered cakes topped with colourful icing or intricate spun-sugar creations. There are no macaron towers where I come from.

Italian bakers take pride in showcasing ancient skills that are passed on from generation to generation and, in respect of this legacy, the recipes are hardly ever altered. The displays at the local pasticceria are nothing less than mouthwatering, though, and the appeal lies in their simplicity. This is where the concept of 'less is more' makes perfect sense. Ingredients are encouraged to fulfil their sweet potential with just the right amount of sugar and other classic ingredients such as flour, almonds and butter. Olive oil is often used in desserts, too, offering a uniquely fruity and piquant aroma and rendering cakes luscious and velvety, like my caprese con nocciole e fragole al vino (chocolate and hazelnut caprese cake with wine-roasted strawberries, see page 252).

When it comes to sweetness, you will not readily encounter sugar-laden desserts or pastries. Such prudent use derives from understanding that the other ingredients are equally important and deserve a chance to shine, too. And so, savoury flavours are often added to sweet creations to restore balance in the baking universe. Such is the case with a much-loved sweet bread from Tuscany, pan di ramerino (sultana, honey and rosemary bread rolls, see page 233), or a traditional focaccia dough topped with cherries and vincotto (see page 239), a triumph of sweet and savoury.

In this chapter you will find a few extra bread recipes, too, some veering to the sweet side, some authentically savoury, although even the crustiest of rolls or the most aromatic rustic loaf can be a vessel for jam or chocolate spread …

CIABATTINE
(MINI CIABATTA BREAD ROLLS)

MAKES 6 OR 8

Ciabatta is one of the most popular Italian breads – its flattened, elongated shape resembling a slipper (ciabatta) and its airy crumb just waiting to be dunked into piquant extra-virgin olive oil. For the ultimate panini, I love to divide a big batch of ciabatta dough into six or eight portions, give them the endearing name of ciabattine (little ciabatta), bake them and slice them in half, then stuff them full of my favourite cheese and cold cuts, such as salami or mortadella.

Combine the flour, 350 ml of water, the olive oil and yeast in a large bowl and mix with a spatula or wooden spoon until the yeast is well incorporated. Add the salt and mix until the dough is soft, sticky and wet. Place in an oiled bowl, cover with a damp tea towel and rest at room temperature for 1 hour or until doubled in size.

Using wet hands, stretch the dough into a rectangle. Fold the top and bottom thirds into the centre, like folding a letter. Place the dough back in the bowl, cover and leave to prove at room temperature until it has almost tripled in size. This will take 8–12 hours, depending on the temperature of the room.

Once the dough has risen, you will notice that lovely air bubbles have formed. These hold the secret to the formation of those coveted holes. Tip the soft and sticky dough onto a floured surface, roll it into a log and cut evenly into six or eight pieces. Place them on a baking tray lined with baking paper, sprinkle with a little flour and dimple the top lightly. Cover and allow to rise for 30–45 minutes or until risen by two-thirds.

Preheat your oven to 220°C. Place an empty metal bowl on the lower shelf of your oven to heat up.

450 g (3 cups) type 00 flour,
    plus extra for dusting
1 tablespoon olive oil
1 scant tablespoon dried yeast
2 teaspoons salt flakes
iced water

Slide the tray onto the middle shelf of your oven, then pour a glass of iced water into the empty bowl to create steam (this encourages a beautiful, even crust and crumb). Quickly close the oven door and bake for 30–35 minutes or until the rolls are golden and the bottom sounds hollow when tapped. You may need to flip the rolls upside down to ensure even baking. Cool on a wire rack before slicing in half to reveal that holey, moist crumb.

PANE DI ALTAMURA
(RUSTIC PUGLIESE-STYLE BREAD WITH SEMOLINA)

MAKES 1 LOAF

Pane di Altamura is one of the most-loved Italian breads all over the peninsula. Its name comes from its place of origin and the type of flour used to create the dense, highly perfumed crumb that keeps soft for days, courtesy of the thick, dark crust that acts as a shield to fend off humidity. Most Italians hardly ever attempt this recipe in their own kitchens, as they know where to find a trusted Pugliese bakery that offers Altamura loaves daily. For immigrants like myself, though, the quest for a traditional, wood-fire baked pane di Altamura is still one to vanquish, so I have created an easier version to make this iconic bread at home. And, while it's not an ancient, authentic Pugliese recipe, it comes close enough that if you close your eyes, you can imagine yourself on those luscious shores.

To make the pre-ferment, mix the flour, yeast and 100 ml of water in a large bowl until a loose batter forms. Cover with a damp tea towel and rest at room temperature for 8–12 hours or overnight.

The next morning the pre-ferment will look bubbly and swollen. Add the flours, yeast and 250 ml (1 cup) of water and mix with a wooden spoon. Sprinkle on the salt and knead vigorously for 5–10 minutes or until the dough is smooth. Transfer to a bowl dusted with durum wheat flour, cover with a damp tea towel and leave to rise for 4–6 hours or until doubled in size.

Turn the dough out onto a floured surface, stretch it into a rectangle, then fold the top and bottom thirds into the centre, like folding a letter, and tuck the ends under to form a ball.

Line a baking tray with baking paper and lightly dust with durum wheat flour. Place the dough on the tray, then cover with a damp tea towel and rest at room temperature for 2 hours or until risen by two-thirds.

Preheat your oven to 220°C. Place an empty metal bowl on the lower shelf of your oven to heat up.

Remove the tea towel, dust the top with durum wheat flour and score with a sharp knife. Slide the tray onto the middle shelf of your oven, and two-thirds fill the empty bowl with iced water to create steam (this encourages a beautiful, even crust and crumb). Quickly close the oven door and bake for 40 minutes or until the bottom of the loaf sounds hollow when tapped and the top is a dark caramel colour. Cool on a wire rack for 1 hour before slicing.

325 g durum wheat flour (semolina flour), plus extra for dusting
100 g (⅔ cup) type 00 flour
½ teaspoon dried yeast
1 scant tablespoon salt flakes
iced water

PRE-FERMENT (BIGA)
150 g (1 cup) type 00 flour
½ teaspoon dried yeast

PAN DI RAMERINO
(SULTANA, HONEY AND ROSEMARY BREAD ROLLS)

MAKES 10

It's hard to tell whether this is a sweet or savoury creation, the combination of honey, sultanas and rosemary has the tantalising potential to be matched with chocolate spread or served with a cheese platter. I simply tend to tear the rolls apart when they are still slightly warm, and the aromas of woody herbs and sweetness still linger in the air, and dunk them in either an espresso or a shot of Vin Santo.

Gently heat the olive oil in a small saucepan over medium–low heat. Add the rosemary sprigs, turn off the heat and allow to infuse.

In the meantime, combine the yeast and lukewarm water in a large bowl and stir with a wooden spoon until the yeast dissolves. Set aside for 5 minutes or until frothy. Add one egg and the honey, strain in half the rosemary-infused oil and mix well. Add the flour, in two or three batches, and incorporate into the mixture by hand. Knead for 10 minutes or until smooth. (Alternatively, you might like to knead the dough in your electric mixer fitted with the dough hook for 4–5 minutes.) Shape the dough into a ball, transfer to an oiled or floured bowl, cover with a damp tea towel and rest at room temperature for 1½ hours or until doubled in size.

Remove the rosemary sprigs from the oil. Add the sultanas and chopped rosemary to the oil and set aside.

Turn the dough out onto a lightly floured surface, knock the air out, stretch it into a rectangle and spread the sultana mixture on top. Roll it into a large sausage shape and cut into ten pieces. Roll each portion into a ball, cover and rest for 1 hour or until risen by two-thirds.

Preheat your oven to 200°C. Line a baking tray with baking paper.

Score the tops of the buns in a noughts and crosses pattern and place on the tray. Lightly beat the remaining egg and brush over the top of the buns. Bake for 20 minutes or until golden.

In the meantime, to make a sugar syrup, combine the caster sugar with 2 tablespoons of water in a small saucepan over medium–low heat. Simmer for 3–5 minutes or until reduced and syrupy.

Take the buns out of the oven and place them on a wire rack. Glaze them with the sugar syrup and allow to cool.

3 tablespoons extra-virgin olive oil

1–2 rosemary sprigs

7 g sachet dried yeast

300 ml lukewarm water

2 eggs

3 tablespoons honey

575 g type oo flour, plus extra
for dusting

100 g sultanas

1 tablespoon chopped rosemary
leaves

80 g (⅓ cup) caster sugar

TIGELLE
(EMILIA-ROMAGNA-STYLE FLATBREAD)

MAKES ABOUT 8

Tigelle are a very typical food of Emilia-Romagna and the easiest way to describe them is to compare them to English muffins. They are made of a yeasted dough, which also gives them the alternate name of crescentine, from the verb 'crescere' (to grow), as the dough needs to rise before it can be cut into rounds and cooked. Traditionally, tigelle are cooked in a tigelliera, a special cast-iron press-pan fitted with 10 cm holes debossed with a floral pattern. Once a disc of dough is placed in each hole and the lid lowered, the dainty stamp is engraved in each tigella.

Tigelle are best served hot, halved and filled with a lardo (lard), rosemary and garlic mixture called 'cunza' (see Note on page 236 to make your own). Good-quality lardo can be rather elusive to find, but luckily tigelle are wonderful with cured meats like mortadella, coppa and salami and soft cheeses like taleggio and stracchino.

If a tigelle press is not in your arsenal of cookware, you can easily cook the tigelle in a frying pan, preferably non-stick and fitted with a lid.

Combine the yeast, lukewarm water and milk in a jug and set aside for about 5 minutes or until frothy. Place the flour and yeast mixture in a bowl and whisk lightly. Add the oil and bring the dough together using a wooden spoon or your hands. Mix in the salt, tip the dough onto a lightly floured surface and knead for 5–8 minutes or until smooth and stretchy. Transfer to an oiled bowl, cover with a damp tea towel and set aside in a warm spot for 2 hours or until doubled in size.

Knock the air out of the dough, then roll out on a floured surface until 5 mm thick. Cut out as many 8 cm or 10 cm discs as you can, rerolling the offcuts as you go. Place the discs on a tray lined with baking paper, cover and rest again for 30 minutes or until risen by two-thirds.

7 g sachet dried yeast

150 ml lukewarm water

2½ tablespoons milk

275 g plain flour, plus extra for dusting

3 tablespoons extra-virgin olive oil

1 teaspoon salt flakes

prosciutto, salami, coppa, thick slices of buffalo mozzarella, stracchino or taleggio, to serve

>

Heat a large non-stick frying pan over medium–low heat. Cook the discs, in batches, for 3 minutes on each side until golden, puffed and cooked through. Transfer to a plate and keep warm. Alternatively, if you have a traditional tigelle pan, season the holes in the pan with oil (use a pastry brush to really get in there), then wipe off the excess with paper towel. Heat the pan on both sides over medium–high heat for 3–4 minutes. Place a dough disc in each hole, press down gently with the pan lid, then cook on both sides for 3–4 minutes, turning halfway through to make sure each side comes into contact with the heat.

Serve warm straight from the pan, cut in half and stuffed with your choice of cold cuts and cheese.

NOTE

If you are lucky enough to find good Italian sliced lardo, you can make cunza by mixing 1 crushed garlic clove with 2 teaspoons of finely chopped rosemary leaves and 2–3 thin slices of finely chopped lardo. This mixture will be enough to flavour the quantity of tigelle this recipe makes – cunza is really a flavouring rather than an abundant filling, as lardo is so rich. Make sure you add the cunza to the freshly cooked tigelle, when they are still steaming inside, to allow the lardo to melt with the residual heat.

FOCACCIA CON CILIEGIE E VINCOTTO
(FOCACCIA WITH VINCOTTO CHERRIES)

SERVES 8

Whether they are found queuing up at their local bakery to secure a warm slice, or have their hands in the dough kneading a homemade batch, it is safe to assume that Italians love focaccia. And while it is true our loyalty lies with the classic Genovese style, dimpled with holes where piquant olive oil happily pools, come harvest time, the Tuscan tradition of topping focaccia with grapes is one we all treasure. In Tuscany they call it schiacciata, but it barely differs from its Ligurian cousin.

This one I am sharing with you is the festive version, dressed to impress with a cascade of ruby cherries delicately kissed by vincotto and olive oil. A sweet and savoury addition to your celebration table.

Combine the yeast and lukewarm water in a jug and set aside for 5 minutes or until frothy. Add the honey and mix well.

If making the dough by hand, place the flour in a large bowl, pour in the yeast mixture and mix with a wooden spoon. Add the olive oil and salt and mix to form a rough dough. Tip the dough onto a floured surface and knead like you mean it for 8–10 minutes or until it is smooth and shiny. If using an electric mixer fitted with a dough hook, place the flour in the bowl, then gradually pour in the yeast mixture, mixing on low speed. Add the olive oil and salt, increase the speed to medium and let the machine turn the sticky mess into a silky dough (this will take about 5–7 minutes). Whichever method you use, the dough should feel slightly sticky. If it seems too wet, add 1 tablespoon of flour and mix it through. Likewise, if it's too dry, add a little olive oil or water. (All flours vary slightly, even within the same brand, and you have to let your instinct guide you.)

Shape the dough into a ball, cover with a damp tea towel and rest at room temperature for 20 minutes. After this time, the dough should be beautifully elastic. Stretch it out to form a rectangle, then fold the top and bottom thirds into the centre, like folding a letter, and tuck the ends under to form a ball. Place the ball in an oiled bowl, cover with a damp tea towel and leave to prove at room temperature for 1½–2 hours or until doubled in size.

7 g sachet dried yeast
380 ml lukewarm water
2 teaspoons honey
500 g (3⅓ cups) plain, type 00 or baker's flour, plus extra if needed and for dusting
2 tablespoons extra-virgin olive oil, plus 2 tablespoons extra for drizzling
3 teaspoons salt flakes
baby basil leaves, to serve

VINCOTTO CHERRIES
1 tablespoon soft brown sugar
400 g fresh or frozen pitted cherries (see Notes)
2 tablespoons vincotto (see Notes) or balsamic vinegar, plus 1 tablespoon extra for drizzling
2 tablespoons extra-virgin olive oil
salt flakes, to taste

>

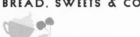

Oil a 30 cm × 20 cm baking dish (or line it with baking paper).

Turn the dough out onto a floured surface and roll out to a 30 cm × 20 cm rectangle. Place in the dish and a press with oiled hands to fit. Cover with a clean tea towel and set aside in a warm place for 45 minutes or until risen.

Preheat your oven to 200°C.

Place all the vincotto cherry ingredients in a bowl, add 2 tablespoons of water and toss to combine.

Gently use your fingers to create dimples in the dough. Scatter the vincotto cherries over the dough, pushing a few cherries into the dimples. Bake for 30 minutes or until the edges are tanned and the top is golden. Remove from the oven and drizzle with the extra olive oil and vincotto or balsamic and scatter on some baby basil leaves. Serve warm or at room temperature.

NOTES

Vincotto is a syrupy condiment made from grape must and is easily available in well-stocked supermarkets; balsamic vinegar is a great alternative.

YouTube taught me a trick to pit cherries: place one over an empty limonata or chinotto bottle and push it down with some force using a chopstick. The pit will fall into the bottle, leaving the pitted cherry ready to use.

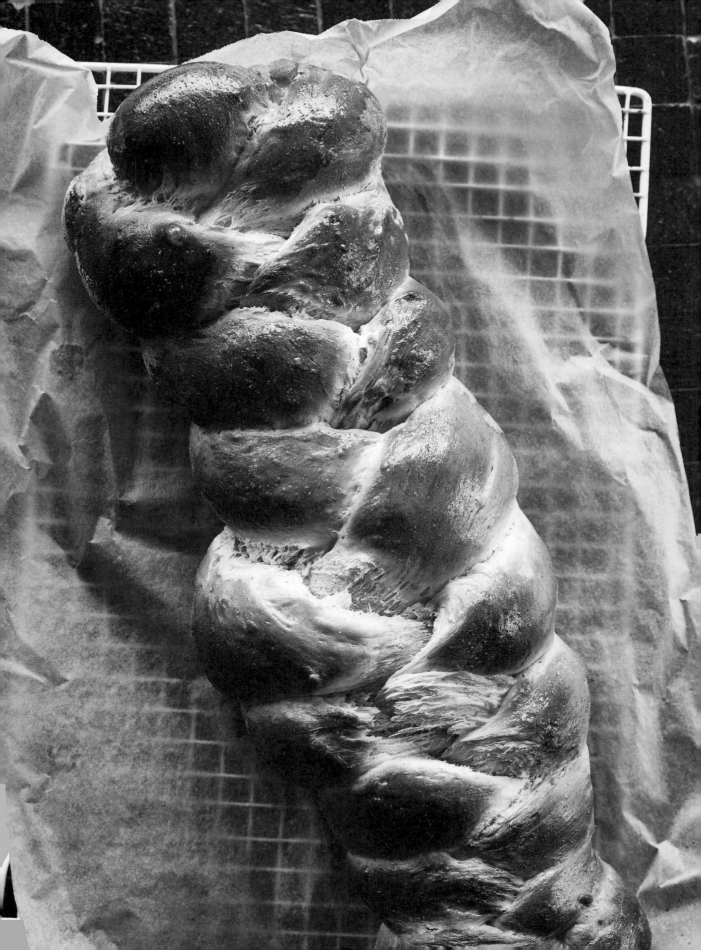

TRECCIA DOLCE
(SWEET EASTER BRAID)

SERVES 6–8

The Catholic tradition of Lent – a time in which lewd behaviour gives way to mindfulness, and excessive eating and drinking is replaced with frugal meals and a strict no-treats policy – comes to an end at Easter. During this time of celebration, kitchens, once again, come to life and become the core of the family. Italian mammas and nonnas don their aprons and busy themselves at the stove, creating food to symbolise spring, fertility and rebirth.

As a child, I would tremble in anticipation for this joyous time to arrive. After 40 long days spent without the wondrous creations my mum had accustomed us to, the time would finally come to rummage in the pantry, reach for the sugar jar and start baking again.

Among the many classic Easter sweets that hold a precious spot in my memory is a special type of orange-scented, enriched bread called treccia dolce (sweet braid). The yeasted dough is built in stages, to encourage an incredibly soft crumb and moist texture. It all starts with a simple ferment made with flour, milk, orange zest and a little yeast, the tangy spark that ignites life for this buttery dough.

I strongly advise you to give your electric mixer a workout when making this bread. The sticky dough needs to be kneaded for a long time before it becomes beautifully smooth and elastic. However, it is perfectly possible to do this by hand, especially if you feel heroic or need to give your upper body a good workout.

To make the ferment, pour the milk into the bowl of an electric mixer and stir in the yeast with a wooden spoon until dissolved. Rest for 5 minutes, then add the honey, flour and orange zest. Mix well with the spoon, cover with a damp tea towel and rest for 1 hour or until doubled in size.

400 g (2⅔ cups) plain flour, plus extra if needed and for dusting

55 g unsalted butter, cubed and softened

2 teaspoons ground cinnamon

100 g caster sugar

2 eggs

butter, jam and chocolate spread, to serve

FERMENT

150 ml lukewarm milk

1 tablespoon dried yeast

1 tablespoon honey

200 g (1⅓ cups) plain flour

finely grated zest of 1 orange

MILK GLAZE

80 ml (⅓ cup) milk

2 tablespoons soft brown sugar

1 teaspoon ground cinnamon

>

Add the flour to the ferment and, using your electric mixer fitted with the dough hook, mix it in on low. Add the butter, a few cubes at a time, and mix it in before sprinkling on the cinnamon and caster sugar. Mix in one egg, then increase the speed to medium and knead for 7–10 minutes or until the dough is smooth and see-through if stretched with your fingers. Add a little flour if it's too wet, or a little water if it's too dry, keeping in mind the dough should feel soft but not too sticky. Shape it into a ball, transfer to an oiled or floured bowl, cover with a damp tea towel and rest at room temperature for 20 minutes or until doubled in size.

Stretch the dough with floured hands into a rectangle, then roll up tightly. Shape back into a ball and return to the bowl, then cover and leave to prove for 2 hours or until almost tripled in size.

Stretch the dough again into a rectangle, then fold the top and bottom thirds into the centre, like folding a letter. Divide the dough into three portions and shape each portion into a rope. Braid the ropes into a long plait, then place it on a baking tray lined with baking paper. Rest, covered with a damp tea towel, for 45 minutes or until risen by two-thirds.

Preheat your oven to 180°C.

Lightly beat the remaining egg and brush over the braid, then bake for 20–25 minutes or until golden.

To make the milk glaze, combine the milk, brown sugar and cinnamon in a saucepan and bring to a simmer over low heat, stirring occasionally, for 2–3 minutes or until the sugar is dissolved and the glaze is slightly reduced.

Brush the milk glaze over the braid and cool on a wire rack. Slice or tear the braid and serve buttered with jam or chocolate spread.

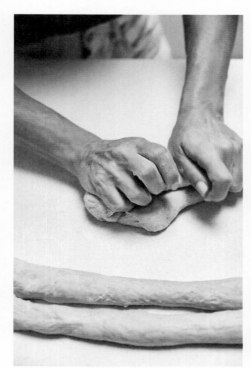

AMARETTI CON MANDORLE CROCCANTI E LIMONCELLO

(LIMONCELLO AND ALMOND BISCUITS)

MAKES 18–20

Amaretti are a quintessential Italian biscuit, with myriad versions appearing all over the country. The common feature these amaretti share is they are a gluten- and dairy-free treat that are, of course, incredibly delicious. The idea behind the recipe is to mix a nut flour, like almond or hazelnut meal, with sugar and egg whites, then add any other flavourings you might like.

I have created many different versions of this versatile biscuit, from hazelnut and chocolate, to almond, coffee and orange, or lemon and vanilla . . . all of them absolutely divine. But, I have to say, these limoncello ones, coated with a shell of crunchy almond flakes, might be my best yet.

Preheat your oven to 180°C. Line a large baking tray with baking paper.

Combine the almond meal and caster sugar in a large bowl. Add the egg whites, limoncello and lemon zest and mix well to create a paste (using your hands is best here).

Pinch off walnut-sized pieces of the paste and shape into a crescent. Roll in the flaked almonds and place on the tray, making sure you leave space between the amaretti.

Bake for 10–12 minutes or until the amaretti look slightly cracked, the flaked almonds are golden and the bottoms are firm. Cool on a wire rack. They will keep for weeks in an airtight container, so you can double the quantities, if you like, and make a bigger batch.

300 g (3 cups) almond meal
250 g caster sugar
2 egg whites
2 tablespoons limoncello
finely grated zest of 1 lemon
65 g (¾ cup) flaked almonds

TORTA DI MELE E MORE
(APPLE AND BLACKBERRY CAKE)

SERVES 8

If I was told I could only have one type of torta for the rest of my life, it would definitely be apple cake. It is my idea of sweet heaven every time I sink my teeth into soft slices of this warm cake. The addition of apple sauce in the batter supercharges the appleness of this tea cake, creating the perfect home for ripe, juicy blackberries.

Preheat your oven to 170°C. Line the base and side of a 20 cm round cake tin with baking paper.

Toss the apple slices in a bowl with the lemon zest and juice and set aside.

In a separate large bowl, whisk the eggs and brown sugar until pale and fluffy. Sprinkle in the salt, sift in the flour and mix well to incorporate. Add the apple sauce and melted butter and stir well, then mix in the apple slices and half the blackberries.

Pour the cake batter into the tin, level with a spoon and top with the remaining blackberries. Bake for 60–65 minutes or until the top is deep golden brown and softly firm to touch. To be sure, insert a skewer into the centre of the cake – if it comes out clean, the cake is ready; otherwise give it another 2–3 minutes and test again.

Allow the cake to cool in the tin for 1 hour, then transfer to a plate and serve with whipped cream.

4 granny smith apples, peeled, cored and thinly sliced

finely grated zest and juice of ½ lemon

2 large eggs

200 g soft brown sugar

pinch of salt flakes

300 g (2 cups) self-raising flour

150 g apple sauce

100 g unsalted butter, melted

125 g blackberries

whipped cream, to serve

SORBETTI FURBI
(NO-FUSS SOFT SERVE SORBETS)

EACH FLAVOUR SERVES 4

This is the most brilliant hack I can share with you: extraordinarily soft and creamy fruit sorbets made with only two ingredients and in seconds. The trick is to choose a fizzy drink – like limonata, aranciata or, my favourite, chinotto – pair it with frozen fruit (berries are always a good idea, as are mango and limonata, lychee and aranciata ... so many amazing options) and blitz it in a food processor until smooth. Then all that is left to do is dollop it into bowls, serve straight away and appreciate a slight sense of smugness.

To make each sorbet, place the frozen fruit in a food processor, pour in the fizzy drink and whiz until smooth and creamy.

Scoop the sorbet into glasses or bowls and serve immediately.

CHERRY AND ORANGE
250 g frozen pitted cherries
125 ml (½ cup) fizzy orange
 soft drink

BLACKBERRY AND CHINOTTO
250 g frozen blackberries
125 ml (½ cup) chinotto

STRAWBERRY AND LEMON
250 g frozen hulled strawberries
125 ml (½ cup) fizzy lemonade

CAPRESE CON NOCCIOLE E FRAGOLE AL VINO

(CHOCOLATE <u>AND</u> HAZELNUT CAPRESE CAKE <u>WITH</u> WINE-ROASTED STRAWBERRIES)

SERVES 8–10

I wouldn't call this decadent cake virtuous, but it certainly is a show-stopping dessert that is criminally easy to make. The addition of wine-roasted strawberries is, if I say so myself, sensational. The alcohol in the wine evaporates, leaving behind sweetness and an elusive mellowness, which matches incredibly well with the richness of the hazelnuts and chocolate. If you add dollops of whipped cream on top before scattering on the strawberries, you can taste paradiso (heaven).

Preheat your oven to 160°C. Line a 20 cm round springform cake tin with baking paper.

Place the chocolate in a large heatproof bowl set over a saucepan of barely simmering water (make sure the bottom of the bowl does not touch the water) and stir occasionally with a metal spoon until melted. Stir in the olive oil and liqueur, then set aside to cool.

Beat the egg yolks and caster sugar in a large bowl until pale and fluffy. Stir in the hazelnut meal, then gently mix in the melted chocolate mixture.

Place the egg whites and salt in a very clean large bowl and whisk until stiff peaks form (feel free to use electric beaters or a stand mixer). Gradually fold the egg whites into the chocolate mixture. Pour the batter into the tin and bake for 40 minutes or until the middle of the cake is slightly wobbly and a skewer inserted into the centre comes out with a few moist crumbs attached. Cool in the tin for 30 minutes, then turn out onto a wire rack to cool completely.

While the cake is cooling, make the wine-roasted strawberries. Increase the oven temperature to 180°C. Place the strawberries, caster sugar, red wine and vanilla seeds in a large bowl and gently toss. Tumble the mixture onto a baking tray and bake for 15–20 minutes or until the strawberries are slightly soft and juicy. Allow to cool to room temperature.

To serve, top the cake with whipped cream, then scatter on the wine-roasted strawberries and their juices just before serving (or the cream will melt).

180 g dark chocolate (70% cacao), broken into pieces

125 ml (½ cup) lightly scented extra-virgin olive oil

1 tablespoon Galliano or Frangelico

4 eggs, at room temperature, separated

230 g (1 cup) caster sugar

250 g (2¼ cups) hazelnut meal

pinch of salt flakes

whipped cream, to serve (or use coconut cream for a dairy-free version)

WINE-ROASTED STRAWBERRIES

500 g strawberries, hulled and bigger ones cut in half

80 g (⅓ cup) caster sugar

2½ tablespoons red wine

1 vanilla bean, split and seeds scraped

FRITTELLE DI MELE CON CREMA PASTICCERA

(APPLE FRITTERS WITH THICK ITALIAN CUSTARD)

SERVES 8

Think soft apple rounds, perfumed with cinnamon and lemon and enveloped in a cloud of fluffy, slightly crisp batter . . . then take the fantasy further and dunk these delights into thick Italian custard. Don't let this be just a fantasy!

To make the Italian custard, heat the milk in a large saucepan over medium heat until just below simmering point. Remove from the heat, drop in the vanilla bean and seeds and lemon zest. Allow to cool for 10 minutes.

In the meantime, whisk the egg yolks and caster sugar in a large bowl until pale and fluffy. Add the cornflour and stir well to remove any lumps. Slowly pour the milk mixture through a sieve (to collect the vanilla bean and zest) into the egg mixture and whisk vigorously to ensure no lumps form. Cook over low heat, stirring gently with a wooden spoon, until it comes to a gentle simmer, then continue to cook, stirring constantly, for 1–2 minutes or until slightly thickened. Remove from the heat and set aside. (The custard can be made a few hours in advance. Cover closely with plastic wrap and refrigerate. Remove from the fridge 20 minutes before serving and stir to loosen it.)

Place the apple in a bowl and toss with the lemon juice.

Beat the egg yolks and sugar in a large bowl until pale and fluffy. Add the flour, cinnamon, lemon zest, Marsala (if using) and 3 tablespoons of the milk and mix to remove any lumps. If the batter is too thick, add the remaining milk.

In a separate very clean bowl, beat the egg whites with the salt until soft peaks form (feel free to use electric beaters or a stand mixer). Fold the egg whites into the batter until smooth.

Pour enough sunflower or vegetable oil into a large heavy-based frying pan to come halfway up the side and place over medium–high heat. Dip the apple rounds in the batter and allow the excess to drip off. Test if the oil is hot enough by dropping in a piece of batter. If it sizzles straight away and bubbles up to the surface, the oil is ready. Working in batches, drop the battered apple rounds into the oil and deep-fry for 3–4 minutes or until golden and fluffy. Remove with a slotted spoon and drain on paper towel. Dust with icing sugar and cinnamon and serve warm with the custard.

3 large firm apples (such as royal gala or fuji), peeled, cored and cut into 5 mm thick rounds
finely grated zest and juice of 1 lemon
3 eggs, at room temperature, separated
1 tablespoon caster sugar
150 g (1 cup) self-raising flour
1 teaspoon ground cinnamon, plus extra for dusting
1 tablespoon Marsala (optional)
60–100 ml milk
small pinch of salt flakes
sunflower or vegetable oil, for deep-frying
icing sugar, for dusting

ITALIAN CUSTARD
400 ml milk
1 vanilla bean, split and seeds scraped
1–2 strips of lemon zest
4 egg yolks
100 g caster sugar
1 tablespoon cornflour

TORTA DI PANE CON CIOCCOLATO E CILIEGIE

(CHOCOLATE AND CHERRY BREAD CAKE)

SERVES 8–10

Torta di pane is a classic Italian cake that beautifully embodies the principles of cucina povera (peasant cooking): simple ingredients, used with knowledge and a touch of thrift. The heft of this dense cake is provided by stale bread soaked in milk until soft. The addition of eggs, olive oil and sugar contribute to building a rich batter that can be flavoured in many different ways. Mum likes to add cocoa, pine nuts and Marsala-soaked sultanas, a really solid flavour combination that I am also partial to. But when cherries are in season, I seek out these ruby jewels to crown this humble cake and transform it into a luscious dessert.

Preheat your oven to 180°C. Line a slice tin with baking paper (the size is up to you – if using a small one, the cake will be taller; if using a larger one, the cake will be flatter and the cooking time a little less).

Soak the bread in the milk in a large bowl and mash it up with your hands until it looks like pulp. The more you reduce it to a pulp, the better the consistency of the cake.

Add the caster sugar, olive oil and eggs to the milk and bread mixture and whisk well. Tip in the flour and baking powder and stir to combine, then mix in the cocoa, Marsala or milk and vanilla. The batter will look runny and a little lumpy (because of the bread).

Pour the cake batter into the tin, place the pitted cherries on top (they will sink into the batter in the oven) and bake for 30–35 minutes (according to the size of your tin) or until the top is puffed and slightly cracked, but there is still a slight wobble in the middle. As it cools down the cake keeps cooking and the top settles. Cool in the tin for 15 minutes, then transfer to a wire rack to cool completely.

While the cake is cooling, place the chocolate in a heatproof bowl set over a saucepan of barely simmering water (make sure the bottom of the bowl doesn't touch the water) and stir occasionally with a metal spoon until melted.

Drizzle the chocolate over the cake, top with some fresh cherries and enjoy.

300 g crustless stale bread

400 ml milk

100 g caster sugar

3 tablespoons lightly scented extra-virgin olive oil

2 eggs

100 g (⅔ cup) type 00 or plain flour

2 teaspoons baking powder

2 tablespoons Dutch cocoa powder

1 tablespoon Marsala (or milk, if you want to keep the cake alcohol free)

1 teaspoon vanilla bean paste or 1 vanilla bean, split and seeds scraped

200 g (1 cup) pitted cherries

100 g dark chocolate (70% cacao), broken into pieces

fresh cherries, to serve

CHIACCHIERE
(FRIED SWEET PASTRY RIBBONS)

MAKES ABOUT 40

These golden, crunchy ribbons of deep-fried sweet dough are a favourite all over Italy, generally enjoyed around Carnevale, the opulent time of year that precedes Lent and the culinary restrictions this religious observance brings. Italy's diversity is reflected in the way this treat is named according to the region you are in. In Milan, where I grew up, and in most of Northern Italy, these sweets are called 'chiacchiere' (chit chat), maybe a reference to the fact that they are offered when friends or neighbours drop in for a quick visit and chat (chiacchiera). They are also known as frappe, crostoli, bugie, cencini or crogetti. Whatever name you wish to call them, my advice is to roll the pastry nice and thinly (a pasta machine will come in handy for this) and commit to deep-frying them. Baking is an option, if you don't love deep-frying, but honestly, probably not worth getting your oven mitts out for.

Place the flour, sugar, eggs and olive oil in a food processor and pulse to create a sand-like texture. Add the alcohol and orange and lemon zests and pulse again. If the dough feels a bit dry, add the milk and pulse again to form a soft and supple dough. This will largely depend on the size of your eggs.

Once the dough comes away from the side of the bowl, lift it out, being careful of the blades. Knead the dough gently on a lightly floured surface for 3–4 minutes or until smooth and similar to a soft pasta dough. It shouldn't be tacky to the touch. Cover with a damp tea towel or beeswax wrap and rest at room temperature for 30 minutes.

Divide the dough into quarters and dust your work surface with flour. Work with one piece at a time and keep the rest wrapped to prevent them from drying out. Flatten the piece of dough with the palm of your hand, then pass it through your pasta machine's widest setting three or four times, folding the dough into three each time. Continue passing the dough through the machine (no further folding required), each time through a thinner setting, until the sheet is 3–4 mm thick. Repeat with the remaining dough.

350 g (2⅓ cups) type 00 or plain flour, plus extra for dusting
80 g (⅓ cup) caster sugar
2 eggs, at room temperature
75 ml olive oil
1½ tablespoons grappa or Marsala (Galliano or Frangelico also welcome), plus extra to serve
finely grated zest of 1 orange and 1 lemon
1 tablespoon milk (optional)
vegetable oil, for deep-frying
icing sugar, for dusting

>

Use a pastry wheel or sharp knife to cut each sheet into 8 cm × 3 cm strips, then cut a slit in the middle of each strip. As the ribbons fry, this helps create a lovely shape.

Pour the vegetable oil into a large heavy-based saucepan to a depth of 4–5 cm and place over medium–high heat. Test if the oil is hot enough by dropping in a little piece of dough. If it sizzles straight away and turns golden in about 15–20 seconds, the oil is ready. Gently drop in 4–5 strips of dough and fry, turning them once, for 15–20 seconds or until deep golden on both sides. Lift the strips out with a slotted spoon and drain on paper towel. Repeat until all the chiacchiere are ready.

Dust the chiacchiere with the icing sugar and serve with grappa or Marsala. Store them at room temperature in an airtight container, where they will keep for up to 5 days.

MARITOZZI
(ITALIAN CREAM BUNS)

MAKES 12

For those who have been exposed to the charming chaos of Rome, where these deep-golden buns brimming with whipped cream are from, maritozzi are a delicious memory you may be keen to recreate at home. They are easy to make, as long as you are willing to knead a brioche-like dough and have enough patience to watch it rise.

The word 'maritozzo' is Roman dialect for marito (husband), and it is said that hopeful boyfriends would hide an engagement ring within the buns and present them to their girlfriends, in the hope to upgrade from fidanzato (boyfriend) to marito. Hard to say no, if you ask me …

Special thanks to my bestie, Jono Fleming, for being the hand model in this shot. That nail polish had to be immortalised!

7 g sachet dried yeast

175 ml lukewarm water

550–600 g type 00 flour

55 g (¼ cup) caster sugar

finely grated zest of 1 orange
    and 1 lemon

3 eggs

pinch of salt flakes

90 g unsalted butter, chopped
    into 1 cm cubes and softened

50 g sultanas, soaked in water for
    30 minutes, then drained well

1 tablespoon milk, lightly beaten
    with 1 egg

GLAZE

50 g caster sugar

CREAM FILLING

600 ml thickened cream

1 tablespoon icing sugar, sifted

1 teaspoon vanilla bean paste
    or 1 vanilla bean, split and
    seeds scraped

Combine the yeast and lukewarm water in a jug and set aside for 10 minutes or until frothy. Place the yeast mixture, 500 g (3⅓ cups) of the flour, the caster sugar, orange and lemon zests and eggs in the bowl of an electric mixer fitted with the dough hook. Knead on low speed for 3 minutes to combine. Add the salt and knead for a further 6–7 minutes or until smooth.

With the motor running on low speed, add the butter, one piece at a time, making sure it is incorporated before adding the next, and mix until smooth and elastic. Add the remaining flour, as needed, to create a soft but not sticky dough. Transfer to a floured bowl, cover with a damp tea towel and set aside for 1½ hours or until doubled in size.

Preheat your oven to 180°C. Line two baking trays with baking paper.

Knock back the dough and knead lightly for 30 seconds, then use your hands to stretch it into a 1 cm thick rectangle. Scatter on the sultanas and roll it into a log, then cut the log into 12 pieces and shape them into ovals. Place on the trays, cover with a tea towel and leave in a warm spot for 30 minutes. Brush the tops with the milk and egg mixture, then bake for 15–18 minutes or until the buns are puffed and deep golden.

While the buns are baking, make the glaze. Combine the caster sugar and 2½ tablespoons of water in a small saucepan over medium–high heat and simmer for 1–2 minutes or until bubbled into a syrup.

Remove the buns from the oven and immediately brush with the glaze, then cool on a wire rack. When ready to serve, whip the cream and icing sugar until firm peaks form. Gently stir through the vanilla. Cut a slit in the middle of the cooled buns, fill with the whipped cream and level with a spatula. Best eaten at once.

BUDINO DI CIOCCOLATO ALL'OLIO DI OLIVA

(OLIVE OIL CHOCOLATE POTS)

SERVES 6

I tend to turn to this simple dessert right after Easter, when the pantry is invaded by ridiculous amounts of chocolate my children really should not eat too much of . . . and so I lend a hand. I steal the coveted dark chocolate eggs and turn them into a grown-up affair with the addition of liqueur, much to my children's dismay. Using olive oil may seem a bit extravagant, but it contributes a delicate, fruity tone and a silky-smooth texture. Just be sure to use a lightly scented one.

Place the chocolate in a large heatproof bowl set over a saucepan of barely simmering water (make sure the bottom of the bowl does not touch the water) and stir occasionally with a metal spoon until melted. Remove from the heat. Add the salt, then slowly pour in the olive oil, whisking continuously. Whisk in the vanilla seeds and Galliano and allow to cool for 5 minutes.

Beat the egg yolks with 115 g (½ cup) of the caster sugar in a separate bowl until pale and fluffy. Add the egg yolk mixture to the chocolate mixture and stir to combine.

Whisk the egg whites in a very clean large bowl until frothy, then gradually add the remaining caster sugar and whisk until soft peaks form (feel free to use electric beaters or a stand mixer). Very gently fold the egg white mixture into the chocolate mixture.

Divide the mixture among six cups or ramekins (or martini glasses for a dramatic effect), cover and place in the fridge to set for 5–6 hours, or overnight. Leave at room temperature for 10 minutes before serving, topped with fresh berries.

400 g dark chocolate chips or leftover chocolate eggs (70% cacao), broken into pieces

pinch of salt flakes

3½ tablespoons lightly scented extra-virgin olive oil

1 vanilla bean, split and seeds scraped

1 tablespoon Galliano (or Frangelico or Marsala)

5 eggs, at room temperature, separated

170 g (¾ cup) caster sugar

fresh berries, to serve

TORTA DI PERE E VINO ROSSO DI MIA MAMMA

(MUM'S RED WINE AND PEAR CAKE)

SERVES 6–8

I am pretty confident that most mammas in Italy have a trusted recipe featuring red wine and pears. Here the match is undeniably appealing – the perfume from the spiced wine mingles with the softness of the pears, which are immersed in a fluffy, ephemerally light batter. This is an impressive dessert when served with some whipped cream and the reduced poaching syrup drizzled on top, or a formidable tea cake, best accompanied by a shot of grappa.

Start by making the poached pears. Place the pear halves snugly in a small saucepan. Add the wine, brown sugar, vanilla bean and seeds and spices and bring to a simmer over medium heat. Reduce the heat to low, cover with a lid of baking paper cut to fit and cook for 45–50 minutes or until the pear is soft. Allow the pear to cool in the poaching liquid.

Preheat your oven to 180°C. Line a 22 cm round springform cake tin or a 40 cm × 30 cm rectangular baking dish with baking paper.

Whisk the eggs and caster sugar in a bowl until pale and fluffy. Add the olive oil, flour and almond meal and mix well.

Remove the pear from the poaching liquid and set aside. Pour 100 ml of the poaching liquid into the flour mixture and gently mix to create a loose batter. Pour the cake batter into the tin, then arrange the pear halves on top, some cut-side up and some cut-side down. Bake for 35–40 minutes or until golden brown and a skewer inserted into the centre of the cake comes out clean. Cool in the tin. Dust with cinnamon sugar to serve.

NOTES

To make your own cinnamon sugar, combine 1 tablespoon of icing sugar with 2 teaspoons of ground cinnamon and mix well.

You can remove the vanilla bean and reduce the remaining poaching liquid for 15–20 minutes or until syrupy. For a decadent dessert, serve the syrup alongside slices of the cake and whipped cream. Or you can go full-on Italian and serve the cooled cake with a shot of espresso or grappa – or both!

3 eggs
100 g caster sugar
75 ml olive oil
170 g self-raising flour, sifted
55 g (½ cup) almond meal
cinnamon sugar, for dusting
(see Notes)

POACHED PEARS

3 william pears, peeled, cut in half
lengthways and cored
500 ml (2 cups) red wine
50 g soft brown sugar
1 vanilla bean, split lengthways
and seeds scraped
1 teaspoon ground cinnamon
½ teaspoon ground cloves

AN ODE TO COFFEE

An Italian's love for coffee is no new mystery unveiled, we famously knock back shots at the counter of our local bar as fast as a formula one car is refuelled at its pit stop. However, coffee in Italy can also be a moment of indulgence, especially when served shaken, with a rich dollop of whipped cream slowly sinking to the bottom of the glass (see opposite), or indeed as one of the main ingredients for Italy's most famous dessert, tiramisù (see page 276). And if you are an affogato devotee (honestly, who isn't?), indulge in creating a cappuccino-flavoured liqueur (see page 273) to liberally pour over a few scoops of gelato.

My absolute favourite Italian coffee habit, though, is that of caffè sospeso; a tradition that sees a generous customer paying for two coffees, one to have and one to leave sospeso (suspended) for someone less fortunate who can't afford to pay for it, but whose daily ritual is not denied. This is what makes our fellow humans so special. This is what food and its consumption is about: sharing, enriching, nurturing.

CAFFÈ SHAKERATO CON PANNA
(ITALIAN-STYLE SHAKEN ICED COFFEE <u>WITH</u> WHIPPED CREAM)

SERVES 4

The name leaves nothing to the imagination, this is Italian iced coffee. Frankly, I often skip the addition of whipped cream and simply enjoy this quintessential summer drink on its own. When coffee is vigorously shaken with ice, the most palatable, airy texture is created, and as you pour it into glasses it elegantly separates into deep dark liquid and foamy caramel top. Must drink in an Italian piazza wearing Gucci sunglasses.

Combine the espresso and sugar (if using). Rest the coffee at room temperature until cool, then put it in the fridge for 1–2 hours.

Combine the cooled coffee and ice cubes in a blender or food processor. Process for 1 minute or until the ice has melted into the liquid.

Whip the cream in a bowl until soft peaks form.

Pour the coffee mixture evenly into four glasses. Top each glass with a dollop of whipped cream and dust with cocoa or cinnamon.

NOTE
If you would like to use store-bought whipped cream from a can, it will be light enough to stay floating on top of the coffee. Freshly whipped cream, however, will inevitably sink into the coffee. Not that this is a bad thing!

160 ml (⅔ cup) freshly brewed espresso coffee (about 4 shots)

2–3 teaspoons caster sugar, or to taste (optional; I actually prefer it without sugar)

5–6 ice cubes

150 ml thickened cream, fridge cold

Dutch cocoa powder or ground cinnamon, for dusting

CREMA DI CAFFÈ
(COFFEE MOUSSE)

SERVES 4

2 tablespoons caster sugar

100 ml freshly brewed
espresso coffee

300 ml thickened cream

50 g dark chocolate chips
(70% cacao)

dark chocolate shavings
(70% cacao), to serve

cookies (such as amaretti or
biscotti), to serve (optional)

Airy and fluffy, with a distinguished soft-serve consistency, crema di caffè is a very popular summer treat, often churned and served at beach kiosks along the Adriatic coast, which is exactly where I long to be …

Add the sugar to the hot coffee and stir to dissolve it. Refrigerate until cold.

Pour the cold coffee and cream into a large bowl and whip with electric beaters on high for 1–2 minutes or until soft peaks form. Gently fold in the chocolate chips.

Transfer the crema di caffè to four coffee cups and top with dark chocolate shavings. Serve with some cookies on the side, if you like.

LIQUORE AL CAPPUCCINO

(CAPPUCCINO LIQUEUR)

MAKES 750 ML

This cappuccino-flavoured vodka is as easy to make as mixing together some espresso, cream and vodka – and such little labour will repay you tenfold in flavour and cheer. Just imagine drizzling liquore al cappuccino liberally over a few scoops of vanilla gelato … next-level affogato!

Place the coffee, cream, milk and caster sugar in a small saucepan over medium–low heat, bring to a gentle simmer (do not boil as it will spill over!) and stir for 1–2 minutes or until the gentle heat melts the sugar. Turn off the heat and allow to cool completely.

Once the mixture is cool, stir the vodka into the coffee cream mixture. Transfer to a bottle and refrigerate overnight. Always shake well before using. Store in the fridge for up to 1 week or freeze for up to 2 months.

NOTE

To serve with gelato, simply scoop some gelato into bowls or glasses and then drizzle liberally with the cappuccino liqueur.

100 ml freshly brewed
    espresso coffee
300 ml pouring cream
100 ml full-cream milk
170 g (¾ cup) caster sugar
200 ml vodka

CIOCCOLATA CALDA AL CAFFÈ CON RIMORCHIO

(HOT CHOCOLATE WITH ESPRESSO AND GRAPPA)

SERVES 2

Caffè con rimorchio (coffee with pick-up truck!) is a typical northern Italian way of pimping up your after-dinner espresso shot with a little cheeky grappa. It is best known all over Italy as caffè corretto (corrected coffee), as if the hard liquor's job is to fix the hot beverage. Imagine adding to this perfect pairing a generous pour of thick, scalding hot chocolate … and you can pretty much predict that any of life's hardships will be fixed, at least for the time it takes to gobble it up.

40 g (⅓ cup) Dutch cocoa powder

80 g (⅓ cup) caster sugar

2 scant tablespoons cornflour

½ teaspoon vanilla bean paste

½ teaspoon ground cinnamon

500 ml (2 cups) milk

80 ml (⅓ cup) freshly brewed espresso coffee (about 2 shots)

2 tablespoons dark chocolate chips (70% cacao)

2 shots of grappa

biscotti, to serve (optional)

Combine the cocoa, caster sugar, cornflour, vanilla and cinnamon in a small saucepan. Pour in 3 tablespoons of the milk and whisk until the mixture turns into a sticky, dark brown paste. Slowly add the rest of the milk, whisking enthusiastically as you go to prevent any lumps from forming. Add the espresso and stir through.

Place the saucepan over medium heat and bring to a simmer, stirring constantly with a metal spoon. Reduce the heat to low, add the chocolate chips and cook, stirring, for about 2–3 minutes or until the hot chocolate starts to thicken.

Remove from the heat, pour into two coffee cups and serve hot, each with a shot of grappa and some biscotti, if you like.

TAZZINE DI TIRAMISÙ
(MINI TIRAMISÙ CAPPUCCINO CUPS)

SERVES 8

3 eggs, at room temperature,
   separated

80 g (⅓ cup) caster sugar

1 vanilla bean, split and
   seeds scraped

500 g mascarpone

pinch of salt flakes

1 scant tablespoon icing sugar

16 savoiardi biscuits

500 ml (2 cups) freshly brewed
   espresso coffee

Dutch cocoa powder, for dusting

dark chocolate shavings
   (70% cacao), to serve (optional)

If the idea of enjoying large portions of creamy tiramisù clashes with your 'everything in moderation' approach to eating, then assembling this iconic dessert straight into cappuccino cups will solve the dilemma. These self-contained little pots are a coffee-lover's pure delight.

Place the egg yolks and caster sugar in the bowl of an electric mixer fitted with the whisk attachment and whisk on medium for 5–6 minutes or until very pale and fluffy. Add the vanilla seeds and whisk well, then gently whisk in the mascarpone, ensuring there are no lumps.

In a separate very clean bowl, whisk the egg whites and salt until soft peaks form (feel free to use electric beaters or a stand mixer). Add the icing sugar and keep whisking for a further 2–3 minutes or until glossy and firm. Gently fold the whisked egg whites into the mascarpone mixture.

Dunk the savoiardi in the coffee (one at a time so they don't go soggy), break them in half and nestle at the bottom of a cappuccino cup. Dollop on a few tablespoons of the mascarpone mixture, then arrange another biscuit, dunked in coffee and broken in half, on top. Cover with another 1–2 tablespoons of the mascarpone mixture. Continue with the remaining ingredients to make eight tiramisù cups. Loosely cover and place in the fridge to set for at least 4 hours, or overnight.

Just before serving, dust generously with cocoa and, if you like, sprinkle on a few chocolate shavings.

CONVERSION CHARTS

Measuring cups and spoons may vary slightly from one country to another, but the difference is generally not enough to affect a recipe. All cup and spoon measures are level.

One Australian metric measuring cup holds 250 ml (8 fl oz), one Australian metric tablespoon holds 20 ml (4 teaspoons) and one Australian metric teaspoon holds 5 ml. North America, New Zealand and the UK use a 15 ml (3-teaspoon) tablespoon.

LENGTH

METRIC	IMPERIAL
3 mm	⅛ inch
6 mm	¼ inch
1 cm	½ inch
2.5 cm	1 inch
5 cm	2 inches
18 cm	7 inches
20 cm	8 inches
23 cm	9 inches
25 cm	10 inches
30 cm	12 inches

LIQUID MEASURES

ONE AMERICAN PINT	ONE IMPERIAL PINT
500 ml (16 fl oz)	600 ml (20 fl oz)

CUP	METRIC	IMPERIAL
⅛ cup	30 ml	1 fl oz
¼ cup	60 ml	2 fl oz
⅓ cup	80 ml	2 ½ fl oz
½ cup	125 ml	4 fl oz
⅔ cup	160 ml	5 fl oz
¾ cup	180 ml	6 fl oz
1 cup	250 ml	8 fl oz
2 cups	500 ml	16 fl oz
3 cups	750 ml	25 ½ fl oz
4 cups	1 litre	32 fl oz

DRY MEASURES

The most accurate way to measure dry ingredients is to weigh them. However, if using a cup, add the ingredient loosely to the cup and level with a knife; don't compact the ingredient unless the recipe requests 'firmly packed'.

METRIC	IMPERIAL
15 g	½ oz
30 g	1 oz
60 g	2 oz
125 g	4 oz (¼ lb)
185 g	6 oz
250 g	8 oz (½ lb)
375 g	12 oz (¼ lb)
450 g	16 oz (1 lb)
1 kg	32 oz (2 lb)

OVEN TEMPERATURES

CELSIUS	FAHRENHEIT	CELSIUS	GAS MARK
100°C	200°F	110°C	¼
120°C	250°F	130°C	½
150°C	300°F	140°C	1
160°C	325°F	150°C	2
180°C	350°F	170°C	3
200°C	400°F	180°C	4
220°C	425°F	190°C	5
		200°C	6
		220°C	7
		230°C	8
		240°C	9
		250°C	10

GRAZIE

Writing a book is a collective effort. I may write the words, test the recipes and cook the food, but without a team of talented creatives behind me, this effort would live as a word document on my laptop and mess in my kitchen.

The Dream Team is led by Mary Small, a woman whose extraordinary zest for life, humour and empathy makes the process of book writing an utter joy. Mary knows how to champion and support her squad, with the intent to make space for all our ideas to be expressed and cherished. My slightly chaotic brain could not be more thankful for such kind, quiet yet knowing leadership. Thank you, Mary, we are so lucky to be captained by you!

My team members are nothing short of extraordinary, and I admire them for their artistry, work ethics and positive 'can do' attitudes: Jane Winning, Megan Johnston and Emily O'Neill, you are a dream to work with!

Vanessa Austin, Rob Palmer and Claire Dickson-Smith, I am so grateful we get to play together every few years, messing up my kitchen and cluttering my front porch with props and photographic equipment! And my neighbours love book shoot days – they always materialise at the end of the filming day with takeaway containers to help us with the leftovers!

Thank you to Jono Fleming, my work hubby ... eight years, nine projects ... I think we are going steady, yes?

Shoot days are a bit of an upheaval for my family life, with rooms taken over by ingredients and tools of the trade, so my biggest thank you goes to my family, my biggest supporters and the people who inspire me to create more recipes and dig deeper into my anecdote archive. Grazie, amore miei!

But my most heartfelt thank you goes to you, dear readers. Your love and support mean the world to me and inspire me to keep telling the story of good, simple home cooking.

x Silvia

INDEX

Pan Macmillan acknowledges the Traditional Custodians of country throughout Australia and their connections to lands, waters and communities. We pay our respect to Elders past and present and extend that respect to all Aboriginal and Torres Strait Islander peoples today. We honour more than sixty thousand years of storytelling, art and culture.

A PLUM book

First published in 2022 by
Pan Macmillan Australia Pty Limited
Level 25, 1 Market Street,
Sydney, NSW 2000, Australia

Level 3, 112 Wellington Parade,
East Melbourne, VIC 3002, Australia

Design, typesetting and illustration by Emily O'Neill
Editing by Megan Johnston
Index by Helena Holmgren
Photography by Rob Palmer
Prop and food styling by Vanessa Austin
Food preparation by Silvia Colloca, Jono Fleming and Claire Dickson-Smith
Colour reproduction by Splitting Image Colour Studio
Printed and bound in China by Imago Printing International Limited

A CIP catalogue record for this book is available from the National Library of Australia.

The publisher would like to thank Marie Louise de Monterey for their generosity in providing clothing for the book.

10 9 8 7 6 5 4 3 2